A Clear Explanation of the Controversy among the Wittenberg Theologians concerning Regeneration and Election

with a refutation of the arguments that Dr. Samuel Huber has thus far brought into the midst of Dr. Aegidius Hunnius, Polycarp Leyser, Solomon Gesner, etc., in defense of his opinion.

Published with the zeal and effort of a man of learning, piety, truth and tranquility who is devoted to the Church.

translated by Rev. Paul A. Rydecki

edited by Rachel K. Melvin

Repristination Press
Malone, Texas

A translation of Aegidius Hunnius, *Controversiae Inter Theologos Wittenbergenses de Generatione et Electione Dilucida explicatio, D.D. Aegidii Hunnii, Polycarpi Leyseri, Salamonis Gesneri, &c. cum refutatione argumentorum quae D. Samuel Huberus pro assertione suae opinionis hactenus in medium attulit*, 1594. Copyright 2012 by Paul A. Rydecki. Published by permission of the translator. No part of this publication may be reproduced, stored in a retrieval system, or transmitted in any form or by any means, electronic, mechanical, photocopying or otherwise without the prior written permission of Repristination Press.

Published in 2013

REPRISTINATION PRESS
P.O. BOX 173
BYNUM, TEXAS 76631

www.repristinationpress.com

ISBN 1-891469-52-5

TABLE OF CONTENTS

To Johann Spies, Typographer in Frankfurt

Most distinguished sir: Many good men, and I as well, have wanted an explanation of that recent controversy that has taken place thus far among the Wittenberg Professors concerning re-generation and a general election of God. And, impatient due to the delay, some have collected a few pages from here and there which mention this litigation briefly, but do not explain it fully. However, immediately following our market day, I happened upon this explanation which is both reliable and, as evident from certain marginal and interlinear marks, is presented by the authors themselves. If you should submit the following explanation to your printing press, you will be doing a great favor to me and to all who are devoted to the truth, and you will be providing a useful service to the whole Church. For the sake of the common good, Dr. Hunnius and the rest of his colleagues neither can, nor should, be reluctant to speak about what this writing of theirs brings to light, even though they themselves are unaware of its publication and have not been consulted. I also understand that some samples of their argument have appeared elsewhere. But I attribute greater reliability to this example that I am sending you because of the censure added by the authors. If you are unable to gratify our desire at this time, either for lack of time or for other reasons, return the original to me as soon as possible so that it may either be transcribed by us or sent to be printed by someone else. Greetings in the Lord. Written hastily from Michelstadt, April 17, 1594.

Your most devoted servant,

Master Samuel Lautenbach

Explanation of the controversy between Dr. Samuel Huber and his colleagues, the theologians at the Academy of Wittenberg.

It should be understood from the beginning what the chief points are that are outside the litigation between us and Dr. Huber, which, in turn, might have come into dispute.

Outside the controversy are these things:

1.   That God seriously "wants all men to be saved and to come to a knowledge of the truth" (1 Tim. 2). We want this to be understood on both sides concerning the entire human race over against the blasphemies of the Calvinists, as also the rest of the Holy Spirit's testimonies say: "As I live, I do not desire the death of the wicked, but that the wicked turn and live" (Eze. 33). "I do not desire the death of the one who dies" (Eze. 18). "The Lord does not want *anyone* to perish, but that *all* should be turned back to repentance" (2 Pet. 3).

2.   That God sent His Son for the whole world, and that the Son was made the propitiation not only for our sins, but also for the sins *of the whole world* (1 John 2). And that He is the Lamb of God who takes away the sin of the world (John 1). Therefore, there never was nor will there be in the future any man for whose sins Christ did not shed His blood, to such an extent that the Scripture plainly affirms that His death was also for the reprobate and perishing (1 Cor. 8, 2 Pet. 2).

3.   That the merit of the Son is seriously offered to all men. "Preach the Gospel to *every creature*" (Mark 16). "Now God commands men that *all people every-*

where should come to their senses" (Acts 17). "Turn to me and you will all be saved—all the ends of the earth" (Isaiah 45). "Come to Me, all you who labor and are burdened" (Mat. 11).

4.   Having placed these questions outside all realm of debate, we now turn to the following matters.

The first matter under controversy:

Whether, just as that will of God, the satisfaction of the Son and the promises of the Gospel are universal, so also election is to be called universal, such as when it is stated that God elected all men equally to eternal life. Huber affirms this; the rest of us, his colleagues, deny it. We will disprove the reasons that he sets forth for his position briefly and in an orderly manner.

Meanwhile, this must be dealt with first: Since both sides agree about the universal will of God for the salvation of men and about that general love of God which Christ mentions in John 3, can this general love and beneficent will of God be called "election," and thus, can it be asserted that God elected the whole world to eternal life?

Response: For our part, we have no desire to quarrel with anyone over words or phrases (as long as the matter itself remains secure and there is no danger near at hand). And for that reason, we do not bring up on charges those who improperly and mistakenly call that "election" which we have called "the merciful will of God." But since Dr. Huber has concluded that the Scripture everywhere teaches a universal election, properly speaking—so much so that he writes that all men, truly, properly and unmistakably have been predestined and elected to salvation; and since he does not wish to acknowledge in any way that he has improperly said that unbelievers, too (Turks, etc.), are elect;

and since he most absurdly interprets those very passages that deal expressly with predestination, such as John 7, Romans 8, Ephesians 1, and, similarly, 2 The. 2, 1 Pet. 1 and 2, to be concerning the election of the whole world to eternal life; since he has not blushed publicly to accuse his dissenters, and especially us, his colleagues, of Calvinism, in spite of all our merit; we could not fail to perform this cleansing in the Church of God, and at the same time come to the aid of the truth in distress and warn about the danger that exists in this new manner of speaking in which he not only states that the whole world was elected to eternal life, but also imagines a general justification in which the whole world has been justified before God, with sin having been remitted and equally forgiven to all men. In fact, he also imagines a general adoption, and also a general sanctification of all men, a regeneration of hypocrites through a Baptism undergone with wicked intent, and other similar things that we will examine in an orderly fashion.

Chapter I: Concerning Election

To explain why we judge this kind of speech—this expression about a general election or predestination to salvation—to be inappropriate, we offer the following reasons.

1.   Because it completely lacks any testimony from Holy Scripture. This will be clearly demonstrated shortly by bringing in all the passages that treat of election or predestination.

2.   Because experience testifies that this improper way of speaking employed by Dr. Huber has afforded an opportunity for horrible blasphemies, so that the adversaries, almost entirely on account of the expressions of Huber, charge our entire Church of teaching such an election and predestination to eternal life, under the embrace of which Cain, Judas, Nero, Heliogabalus, and others who are more monsters than men, lie in wait to be included. Since the doctrine is misrepresented, simple minds are offended by these accusations, and those who could have been won end up being alienated. Such a pattern of sound words is rightly preferred and urged that is not susceptible to charges of this kind. Nor should anyone claim that no consideration should be given to the adversaries, since they are accustomed to corrupting and perverting even the most correct statements with their distortions. Indeed, we are not unaware of this. But meanwhile, it must be seen that, by giving birth to and defending, expressions that are less congruent with the sound pattern of words, we ourselves are providing our adversaries with occasion for slander, while putting an obstacle before our brothers. And we know how important it is not only to avoid giving offense, but, as much as possible, also to avoid taking offense.

3.   Even less does it seem wise to use this expression of which we now speak, now that Franciscus Puccius has built up his profane dogma from this false premise of some universal election of all men and of their inscription in the Book of Life, to the deception and detriment of the whole Christian faith.

4.   Because this new form of speech forces one to retreat from the long-standing doctrine of our instructors—of Luther and of other most distinguished theologians of the Augsburg Confession who did not teach an election that pertains equally to all mortals, but that which we teach, which has in view only believers and those who remain constant in faith until the end. And to what end is it advantageous to import improper forms of speech when there are proper ones at hand? Certainly nothing is gained with these improper forms of speech other than that the very article is obscured and wrapped in equivocations, so that it becomes less clear to whom the Scriptures truly refer as the elect.

5.   Finally, since both by subscription and solemn vow we are obliged to retain the doctrine that was approved by consensus of the Church and set forth in the Book of Concord, there is a very powerful reason for us not to extend election universally to all men, but rather individually, to believing children of God only. For this is what the Epitome of the Book of Concord says: "The predestination or eternal good pleasure of God *only* pertains to the good and beloved children of God."[1] And then shortly afterwards: "The Word of God leads us to Christ. He is that Book of Life in whom all those who *obtain* eternal salvation have been inscribed and elected. For this is what is written: 'He elected us in Christ before

---

1   FC:Ep:XI:5

the foundation of the world.'"[2] And again: "In Christ, therefore, the eternal election of God the Father is to be sought. He decreed in His eternal counsel that He desires to save *no one* except for those who acknowledge His Son Jesus Christ and truly believe in Him."[3] Again the Book of Concord says this: "The eternal election or predestination of God to salvation *does not at the same time* pertain to good and evil, but *only* to the children of God, who have been elected and ordained, even before the foundations of the world were laid, to reach eternal life, as the Apostle testifies, saying, 'He predestined us in Him for the adoption of sons through Jesus Christ.'"[4] And again: "Therefore, as we noted above, *no one* should *by any means* conclude that those also are to be reckoned among the number of the elect who despise, cast away, curse and persecute the Word of God, etc."[5]

Therefore, since this is the received and subscribed doctrine of our churches, let us hold that the will of God by which He wants all men to be saved is certainly universal; but that election is not universal of all men, but of all believers, and thus particular with respect to the world.

For if I may pursue this thread, there is a certain universality to God's election, yet not the kind that extends to unbelieving and impenitent men or peoples. Rather it extends to *all* true believers in Christ Jesus. A universality of this kind belongs to these sweetest and truly evangelical promises. "*Everyone* who believes in Him does not perish, but has eternal life" (John 3 and John 6). "Truly I say to you, *whoever* believes in Me has eternal life." Romans 3, "The righteousness of God through faith in Je-

2   FC:Ep:XI:7 (Latin - ... *in quo omnes inscripti et electi sunt, qui salutem aeternam consequuntur.*)
3   FC:Ep:XI:13
4   FC:SD:XI:5
5   FC:SD:XI:39

sus Christ upon *all* and over *all* those who believe." And Romans 9, "Everyone who believes in Him is not put to shame." Anyone who denies that these propositions are truly universal should be sent back to the rudiments of dialectics, even though the propositions themselves do not embrace all men indiscriminately, but rather all those who are included in its scope, which is unmistakably shown by the limitation that is added to them. Since this very universality has in view *all* who are truly believers in Christ Jesus, we say that election is also truly universal. However, it is called particular—not that there is some other universal election in relation to which this election is called "particular," as Dr. Huber ineptly argues, quite the same as if someone were to gather from the saying of Christ, "Few are chosen," that, therefore, all are chosen. For that would be contrary to the laws of dialectics, to reason from the particular to the universal. But it is called particular because it does not refer to all men, but only to those who are in Christ Jesus our Lord. Therefore, if one considers the grammatical meaning, then this particularity agrees with election, since not the whole world, but part of the world—that is, those who believe—are the elect. Or, if one wishes to follow the rules of dialectics and take into account the proposition of Christ, "Few are chosen," as well as Paul's statement that, "Not many are chosen" (1 Cor. 1), then it is an established fact that this proposition is particular, not universal. But neither its "fewness" nor its particularity stands opposed to the universality of the promises, as the Calvinists prattle, but it is made subordinate. And of course, if that universal mercy and will of God were the entire cause for establishing the election of men, with no other attendant cause being added to effect a restriction, then of course, just as that will of God is universal and has the entire human race in view, so for the same reason, election would also be properly called "universal."

But now, since that general love and mercy of God is not

the entire cause, but other things are required in addition for the establishment of divine predestination, namely Christ, in whom election was made (Eph. 1)—and indeed, Christ, not as He is considered apart from faith and disengaged from saving us, but as apprehended by faith—the result is that it is not permissible to state the same thing regarding election that one may state in this matter concerning the merciful will of God.

The matter may become clearer with another example. That mercy and goodwill and love of God is no less a cause of justification than it is of election (Eph. 2, etc.). And certainly if it were the entire cause, so that, in order to effect justification, no other causes were required, then, to be sure, justification would extend just as widely as that mercy and gracious will of the Lord extends. But now other causes come into play that render justification more restricted than that general love and mercy of God are, inasmuch as man does not end up sharing in it except by faith[6].

Hence it is also easy to respond to the question of what the intention of God is toward us. For when it is thus argued, "The intention of God in His eternal good pleasure was that the whole world should be elected. Therefore, the whole world was elected," the antecedent line of thought[7] requires some explanation. For it cannot be so simply stated. For since the election of God was done according to foreknowledge (1 Pet. 1) and yet God foreknew in His eternal counsel that most people would not believe, therefore the Book of Concord rightly states that, for this very reason, God's intention toward them was that they should not be elected, but that they should be judged and condemned as those who despise the grace of God.

The next point in this line of thought is out of place, since it is not permissible to argue from the intention alone toward the

---

6   *ut pote cuius non nisi per fidem homo compos evadit*
7   *Enthymematis*

fulfillment, because the argument cannot proceed due to an insufficient enumeration of causes. Otherwise, one would have to conclude from the institution of the Ministry and from the individual parts of it that all men are thus converted and saved:

> Since God institutes the Ministry of reconciliation and commands that the Gospel be preached to the whole world (Mark 16), He directs His intention to this, that the whole world should be converted and saved.
>
> ***Therefore, the whole world is converted and saved.***

Likewise:

> Baptism was ordained so that, by reason of the intention and institution of God, it may be a washing of regeneration.
>
> ***Therefore, all are regenerated, not only infants (for it is certain that they are regenerated) but also hypocrites who, in their hypocrisy, are baptized at an adult age.***

Similarly:

> God directs and destines the Sacrament of the Lord's Supper to this end, that men may feast on this banquet for eternal life.
>
> ***Therefore, all who use this Sacrament feast on it for eternal life, nor does anyone eat or drink for judgment.***

These are mere paralogisms that arise from an insufficient enumeration of causes.

Indeed, what is the point of teaching either two elections or two predestinations to one eternal life—one universal, the other particular, both of which were made from eternity? One of these, namely, the universal one, can be rendered void in the end. But the other one, which we teach, remains unchanged. In the former, God would write all men into the Book of Life, but in the latter, He would consign only those who were going to believe in Christ Jesus. And in turn, He could blot out on account of foreseen unbelief those whom that general predestination of God had inscribed. By this reasoning, God is supposed both to have inscribed those men (that is, the reprobate) from eternity by virtue of a general predestination, and, without any intermission, to have crossed them out by virtue of the condemnation that takes their unbelief into account—as if we were to think of some sort of predestination that was not made with any forethought toward believers, but as if by a blind will toward all people, in whatever state they may be found, even though God undoubtedly "predestined according to foreknowledge" (as Peter says) "those whom He foreknew" (Rom. 8), namely, those whom He foreknew would be continually believing in Christ Jesus unto the end, even as St. Augustine has left us an elegant and scholarly explanation of this foreknowledge in his Treatise 42 on John.

To be sure, if we set aside these preconceived notions and wish to evaluate such lofty matters with a right judgment, then we must admit that the Scriptures recognize only one predestination of God to one eternal life—the one described in the Word of the Lord in such a way that it cannot be ascribed to those who either never will believe or who were not going to persevere continually until the end.

First Argument that election is not to be ascribed broadly to all men

Certainly the very word "election" demonstrates this clearly, meaning to select and separate something out of a number, a multitude, a crowd or a mass. No one should repudiate this grammatical meaning of the vocable, inasmuch as it is most clearly affirmed and strengthened in this very pinnacle of doctrine with the approval of both Moses and Christ. Indeed, Moses says in Deu. 7: "The Lord has chosen you from *all the nations* of the earth to be for Him a special people." Similar sayings can be read in Deu. 10, 26 and 32, as well as 1 Kings 8: "You have *separated* them for Yourself from *all the peoples* of the earth as an inheritance." Again, Christ, in John 15, likewise urges this grammatical meaning, saying: "*I have chosen you out of the world.*" And this expression has been received in our churches, that "God elects and gathers an eternal Church *out of the human race.*"

Argument #2

Also testifying to this are the titles with which the orthodox writers, both ancient and modern, discuss this article concerning election, calling it not the election of all men, but the election or predestination of the *saved, of the saints, of believers*. Nor will Huber be able to come up with anyone who will ever create such a title for this article, promising to speak of an election of the entire human race.

Argument #3

Indeed, Christ Himself not just once, but twice affirms that many are called, but few chosen.[8] Paul casts his lot with

---

8   *electos*

Christ, affirming that God did not choose many who were wise according to the flesh, not many who were strong or noble by birth. But it has been demonstrated elsewhere that the reason for this paucity does not reside in the will of God, but in men. Nor do we rebuke the adversaries simply for teaching that election is particular, but because they shamefully thrust the reason for the paucity of the elect back onto God Himself and His absolute decree which they imagine He made concerning the damnation of the majority of men. We also rebuke them because they restrict their version of election to these or to those persons who are considered simply and indiscriminately, saying that they absolutely must be converted and saved.

Argument #4

And since Paul teaches in Eph. 1 that our election is founded in Christ, and that we were elected in Him, how, then, can those who are not in Christ be considered in the number of the elect? Surely no one is in Christ apart from faith! Therefore, election is not of all people, but only of believers—of those who remain in Him by faith.

Argument #5

And what can be more powerful or clearer for confirming this point than the fact that Christ so clearly distinguishes between the world and the elect? Consider what He says in John 15: "I have chosen you out of the world." And in John 17, how many times does He distinguish between the world and the elect? "I have revealed Your name to the men whom You gave Me out of the world. I do not pray for the world, but for those whom You gave Me. They are not of the world, just as I also am not of the world." These and many other things plainly separate the elect from the rest of the cesspool of unbelievers and wicked men. And they most clearly prove that not the entire world is elect, but out of the whole world, believers in Christ are elect.

Argument #6

That unique chain of events in St. Paul can expedite the whole matter when he says: "Those whom He foreknew, He also predestined; those whom He predestined, He also called; those whom He called, He also justified; those whom He justified, He also glorified." Therefore, none are predestined to life except for those who were foreknown (that they should be in Christ through faith), and none are predestined according to foreknowledge (1 Pet. 1) except for those who are called. Therefore, outside of the assembly of the called, that is, the Church, the elect are not to be sought. Again, none are predestined, except for those who are also justified. And none are predestined except for those who are finally glorified.

Argument #7

In addition, whenever the Scriptures call people elect and predestined, all of these people are said to come to faith in Jesus Christ. There are many clear testimonies that support this. John 6: "*Everything* that My Father gives Me comes to Me." John 10: "You do not believe," says Christ to the Jews, "because you are not of the number of My sheep, even as I said to you, 'My sheep hear My voice, and I know them, and they follow Me.'" And a little earlier: "I know My sheep and I am known by them." Similarly Acts 13: "As many as were preordained to eternal life believed." This is so true that Paul writes to the Thessalonians that they were chosen "in faith of the truth" (2 The. 2), which points to this very thing, that faith was included in the mystery of election—not, to be sure, by reason of its worthiness or merit, as if it were some sort of virtue or quality dwelling in us, but almost as if it goes outside itself and apprehends Christ Jesus as the rock of our eternal predestination. Thus, Titus 1 assigns faith as the proper sign of the elect, calling it "the faith of God's *elect*."

Whence this argument again emerges for us: The elect of God have faith (Titus 1), and indeed *all* the elect have faith, which the cited testimonies teach. But not all men have faith (2 The. 2). Therefore, not all men are elect, especially not *properly speaking*, as Huber most ineptly contends.

Argument #8

All the elect will be saved.

But not all men will be saved.

Therefore, not all men are elect.

The major premise of this syllogism is also clear from the previously mentioned saying in Romans 8: "Those whom He predestined, He also *glorified*." It is additionally proved from the clear testimony of Daniel 12: "At that time, your people will be saved, *everyone* who is found written in the book." Concerning this, the Scriptures call "elect" the same ones who are written down in heaven (Luke 10, Heb. 12). They are called "heirs of the kingdom" (James 1) for whom the kingdom has been prepared from the beginning (Mat. 25), who will be heirs of salvation (Heb. 1). And those whom Paul in Romans 9 solemnly declares to be the remnant *of the saved*, according to what was said in Isa. 10: "Even though the number of the sons of Israel were like the sand of the sea, *the remnant will be saved*." The Apostle calls them the remnant according to the *election* of grace (Rom. 11). This collection of Scripture passages is like a finger pointing out that the elect are the very ones who are also saved, and *vice versa*.

Argument #9

A similar argument is also gathered from other passages of Scripture that are just as clear:

As many as were elected do not perish eternally, but persevere in faith continually to the end.

But many perish and do not persevere in faith.

Therefore many (by their own fault) were not elected.

The major premise is founded on Matthew 24, where it says that it is impossible for the elect to be led into error, that is, it is impossible that they should persevere in an error that overturns the foundation of salvation so that they perish. Therefore, the Savior indicates that God elected those who remain firm and steadfast in the true faith in the face of all seduction of errors. Thus in John 6 it says: "This is the will of Him who sent Me, the Father, that I should lose nothing of *all* that He gave Me, but that I should raise them up on the last day." "My sheep hear My voice; and I know them, and they follow Me; and I give them eternal life, and they will not perish eternally, nor will anyone snatch them out of My hand." (John 10)

Indeed, Paul preaches forcefully about the elect in Romans 8: "It is impossible that they should be separated from the love of God that is in Christ Jesus our Lord." "For the foundation of God stands *firm*, having this seal: 'The Lord knows those who are His'" (2 Timothy 2).

Argument #10

Certainly if, in the fear of God, we search in the Holy Scriptures, they define election and the predestination of God for us, not as something that can be rendered invalid and fail to reach its intended goal, but as such an election that achieves the ultimate goal of the salvation of souls, and so, through the ordained means, leads from its first origin (which is the grace of God) all the way through to the very end. For this reason, then, election is called predestination or "predetermination"[9] from the end itself, προόρισμός in Greek. If the end is not reached, but is interrupted, it loses its name and definition, so that it is not a προόρισμός or a predetermination and predestination to the end.

We have a sure witness in this matter—the Apostle Paul, who says to the Romans in chapter 11: "What then? What Israel sought (namely, salvation), they did not gain. The elect gained it, but the rest were blinded." We also have the Apostle Peter who affirms that those who were elected according to the foreknowledge of God the Father are guarded by the power of God through faith for salvation, and reach the goal of faith, the salvation of souls (1 Pet. 1).

Argument #11

Whenever mention is made of the remnant, an obvious separation from the remaining multitude is indicated. But the elect are called *the remnant* according to the *election* of grace (Rom. 11). They are called the holy seed *who remained* in Zion, *those remaining* in Jerusalem (Isa. 4), purchased from among men, the firstfruits to God and the Lamb (Rev. 14). Therefore, let them be physically separated from the rest of the multitude of the reprobate and unbelieving and impenitent. Consequently, it is taught contrary to the doctrine of the Holy Spirit when someone also raises unbelievers up to the status of the elect, especially when a person contends, as Huber does, that all men, including unbelievers, are *properly* elected.

9   *praefinitio*

Argument #12

But I shall proceed.

> None of the elect will stand on the last day at the
> left side of the Judge. Nor will they be sent away
> with the devils into the eternal fire by sentence of
> the supreme Judge, Christ.
>
> But all the impenitent and unbelieving will stand
> at His left and will go into the eternal fire.

***Therefore, none of those who are finally impen-
itent and unbelieving were elected.***

Anyone who denies the major premise confuses the two
very distinct groups of elect and damned. He further rejects the
common and well-known prayer of Christians in which, up until
now, they have been accustomed piously to pray for their friends
who have died in Christ, that they may take part in the blessed
resurrection together with ***all the elect.*** That prayer will have to
be corrected, if, based on the Huberian dogma concerning the
election of all men, those also are to be numbered among the
elect who will rise to damnation, who will be tortured with the
devil for all eternity.

But that the truth of the major premise in our syllogism
may be clearly elucidated, the testimonies of the Holy Spirit
must be again noted. In the description of the Last Judgment, it
is read that Christ will send His angels to gather ***His elect*** from
the four winds, from the heights of the heavens from one end
to the other (Matthew 24). And in chapter 25, He calls those
very elect the sheep that are to stand at His right, clearly just as
Christ identified the elect as His sheep in John 10. Concerning
the damned who will stand at His left and will go into the eternal
fire, the Scriptures affirm that they are neither elect nor are they

written in the book of life (Rev. 20). He who is not found written in the book of life will be hurled into the fiery flame.

Argument #13

But take this argument as well:

All the elect are sanctified in time.

The impenitent, especially those who are outside the Church, are not sanctified in time.

Therefore, such impenitent are not the elect.

Isaiah's saying in chapter 4 provides the evidence for the major premise. "Everyone who is left in Zion and who remains in Jerusalem will be called *holy, everyone* who is written in the records of Jerusalem."

Argument #14

Another compelling argument can be constructed in favor of our conclusion from Colossians 3.

The elect of God are clothed in tender compassion, kindness, modesty, meekness, mildness.

The impenitent are not like this.

Therefore, neither are the impenitent among the elect.

Argument #15

Again:

All the elect of God are sons of God.

None of those who finally persevere in sins are sons of God.

Therefore, none of those who are finally impenitent are among the elect.

The major premise is confirmed by authority of the Epistle to the Romans, chapter 8, where he calls those same ones elect whom he had previously designated as sons in the same context, crying, "Abba, Father!" as they await the adoption, the redemption of their bodies. Then it is also proven from the first chapter of the Epistle to the Ephesians: "He predestined us for the adoption of sons." But now, that right to become children of God belongs to believers only, that is, to those who believe in the name of Christ (John 1). Therefore, only these were predestined and elected to eternal life.

Argument #16

Any who lack the wedding garment are not to be considered as the elect.

All unbelievers lack the wedding garment.

Therefore, they cannot be considered to be among the number of the elect, as long as they are and remain unbelievers.

The major premise is well-known from the parable in Matthew 22 where the sentence of reprobation and ejection into outer darkness is rendered concerning the hypocrite because he is not dressed in the wedding garment. This very reason is added: "For many are called, but *few* are *chosen*[10]."

Argument #17

The Apostle exclaims concerning the elect in Romans 8, "Who will accuse the elect of God? God is He who justifies." Hence this immovable foundation of our doctrine is established.

The elect of God are justified, so that no crimes can any longer be charged against them. But the unbelievers are neither justified (because, of course, they lack faith in Christ, by which alone men are justified), nor are their crimes hidden so as not to be charged against them. For they remain subject and liable to eternal damnation (John 3).

Therefore, it is absurd to place those who lack faith into the class of the elect. But it is even more absurd to say that such people are elected to life by an election that is properly so called, even as Dr. Huber constantly insists that all men are simply called "elect," not improperly, but properly speaking.

Argument #18

All the elect have been written in the Book of Life (for to be elected and to be inscribed in the Book of Life are indisputably linked).

But now, wicked men who fight against Christ are not written in the Book of Life.

Therefore, they are not elected, and consequently it should be considered false to say that all men are elected.

The minor premise clearly depends on the testimony in Revelation 17. "The inhabitants of the earth will be amazed at the beast—all those whose names are not written in the book of life from the *creation of the world.*"

Argument #19

Furthermore, if all men equally were indiscriminately elected and predestined to eternal life, then the antithesis that the Scriptures place between elect and non-elect would be out of place. But since the Scriptures clearly discern between elect and non-elect, that certainly testifies that not all have been elected indiscriminately, but only those have been personally elected who believe in the Son of God. This antithesis is manifest from the following, as Matthew 24 distinguishes by way of antithesis between the seductive reprobate, the false prophets and false christs on the one hand, and the elect on the other, who do not allow themselves to be led into their error. Thus John 10: "You do not believe because you are not of My sheep." John 13: "I am not speaking about all of you; I know those whom I have chosen." Romans 11: "What then? What Israel sought, it did not obtain, but the elect obtained it. But the rest" (who are not included in election because of their unbelief) "were blinded." In 2 The. 2, after he has discussed those who perish because they did not believe the truth but approved of injustice, he immediately adds by way of clear antithesis: "But we should always give thanks to God for you, brothers loved by the Lord, because God elected us to salvation from the beginning." The antithesis between elect and non-elect is just as clear where Paul, in 2 Timothy 2, most clearly separates Hymenaeus and Philetus from the number of the elect—since they had wandered from the truth, saying that the resurrection had already happened—and had shipwrecked their faith. These things are said thus far concerning the reprobate. What follows concerns the elect: "Nevertheless, the solid foundation of God stands, having this seal: The Lord knows those who are His."

Thus in 1 Peter 2: "To those who do not believe, the stone that the builders rejected has begun to be the capstone, and a stone over which men stumble and a rock at which they take offense," referring, of course, to those who stumble over the Word and do not believe in it, for which they also had been prepared. Thus far concerning the reprobate. Now follows by way of antithesis: "But you are a *chosen*[11] race, a royal priesthood, a holy people, etc." These and other similar antitheses—of which the Revelation of John is full, where some are sealed, others not sealed, where many are written in the Book of Life, but many are not written, etc.—plainly argue that not all men can be proclaimed to be elected. Rather, it is necessary to preserve a real yet hidden difference between these and the reprobate (who, nevertheless, are condemned by their own fault).

Argument #20

Finally, since Paul also teaches about condemnation and the reprobate whom God casts away because of their final impenitence, and clearly distinguishes between the vessels of mercy and the vessels of wrath, then certainly, if the election of all men were to be alleged, then the one making such an allegation would be proved guilty of manifest falsehood by Paul's doctrine concerning the reprobate. In turn, if the doctrine concerning the condemnation of unbelievers stands, then it is necessary that Huber's doctrine concerning the predestination of all men to salvation, even unbelievers, must fall. For since both election and its counterpart, condemnation, were determined[12] from eternity, so that the Book of Concord says that "God decreed in that same eternal counsel of His (by which He purposed to save believers in *Christ*) that He wished to harden, reject and condemn those who despise the Word and who spurn the grace of the Holy Spirit," certainly all those who lie under this condemnation (because of this foreseen unbelief) have now been separated from the grace of predestination (on account of this unbelief of theirs).

---

11   *electum*
12   *facta*

Therefore, to assert concerning those same reprobate that they were predestined from eternity to salvation through a universal election, and that the same people were rejected from eternity through condemnation in the way here described, is to establish a true contradiction, and to shatter that eternal mystery of predestination by means of a paradox that has now been completely and thoroughly exposed.

Argument #21

The following rule has been well-worn and received in the schools of these regions for some time now: *Outside the visible assembly of the Church, that is, the called, none are to be imagined to be among the elect.* Huber wishes to erase this rule with a single stroke, pronouncing that, as he himself says, they are also properly the elect who are outside the Church, outside the assembly of the called—even those who furiously and viciously attack this assembly of the called and the Church of Jesus Christ. Our children learn this rule about the elect not being sought outside the assembly of the called from the *Dialectic* of Philip Melanchthon. For these things are read in his treatment of the second type of syllogisms:

> The elect are only in the assembly of the called, that is, it is necessary that those who are elect be in the assembly of the called, that is, of those who are baptized and embrace the Gospel. Hence this syllogism is extracted which contains the doctrine and the sweetest comfort.

> The elect are only in the assembly of the called, as Paul says, "Those whom He elected, He also called."

> No Mohammedans are in the assembly of the called.

Therefore, none of the elect remain among the Mohammedans.

These, indeed, are the arguments on which we based our conclusion. Let Huber, in turn, demonstrate *a single* testimony of Scripture by which the word "election" or "elect" (meaning the election to salvation) encompasses all men broadly and indiscriminately, and not rather those only who by way of antithesis are set against the reprobate, although they are reprobate not by an absolute decree of God, but through and because of their final foreseen unbelief and impenitence. For if he were to set forth any testimony by which election or the title of the elect could be accommodated to all mortals under the sun, even to those who will never believe in the Son, then we would no longer resist him in the least.

For the passage in Eph. 1 is restricted by Paul himself to the saints and believers in Christ Jesus, and there the election is defined with respect to Christ—Christ as He is known and laid hold of by faith. But regarding the things that he adduces concerning that will of God, of the love and philanthropy of God toward all men, the response is given above: that the causes should not be confused with the effects, nor should one argue from an insufficient enumeration of causes. Let Dr. Huber speak in accordance with the Scriptures and call the will of God "the will of God." Let him call love "love." And let him not confuse those things that, even though they be combined in his own mind, demand nevertheless a necessary distinction.

If he is going to treat of election, let him not transpose his starting point and ending point, nor let him exchange the *terminus*, or rather, the foundation from which election arises, with the *terminus* at which election aims. Nor let him confuse the beginning and the end, but rather, let him permit each one to remain in its own respective place and order. We offer this admonition because he is accustomed to calling predestination the election to grace, using the word "grace" to fool his readers. For this form of speech seems more plausible to him and more acceptable to the simple whom he wishes to entice, to say that all men are predestined and elected "to the grace of God." That we may expose this fallacy, it must be held that the grace of God (if we would speak from the foundation of Scripture) is not the goal or the *terminus* of election or predestination, *to which* election brings a person, but rather, it is the beginning, cause and source *from which* election flows and arises. Therefore, by the grace of God, beginning with our predestination in Christ, as it were, we were predestined to the goal of election, which is salvation and eternal life and the inheritance of the sons of God in the heavenly kingdom. It is also for this reason that predestination is called προορισμός in Greek, that is, a predetermining[13], being considered from the end which the predestination reaches by the grace of God, considered through its means, and directed to that ultimate end which is, for God's part, His glory, and for our part, eternal life.

Hence it is apparent what response ought to be given to the comparison proposed by Dr. Huber when he says, "The whole world couldn't have been loved by God unless the whole world had been elected and predestined to this love of God. Therefore, election precedes, in logical order[14], the love of God." But here Dr. Huber again confuses cause and effect. For that love of God is not the effect of election, but rather the cause of it, and for that reason, logically comes first, to such a degree that, as all sound theologians agree, the same things are said to be the causes of election which are the causes of justification, among which the

13   *praefinitio*
14   GREEK: τάξει

love and grace of God is first and foremost as the primary and supreme cause of our predestination to life. But Dr. Huber stumbles over the aforementioned boulder at the same time, by confusing the *terminum a quo* with the *terminum ad quem*, as was demonstrated a little earlier.

Among his fallacies is also this: whenever the sayings either of Scripture or of the writers of the Church oppose him— when they teach that predestination pertains only to those who persevere and remain believers in the Son until the end—, his immediate response is usually that "those sayings only have to do with individual election[15] and do not, for that reason, overturn the universal election." So it is that he imagines the logical sequence constructed from the testimonies of the Holy Spirit in the *Theses* of Dr. Hunnius to be single-handedly destroyed with his Pythagorean "I deny it!"[16] Since, then, Dr. Huber denies it, shall we simply acquiesce to his denial? But he does not address the crux of the argument which I (Hunnius) demonstrate by induction in my theses, that ultimately, whenever any mention is made in all of Scripture concerning the salvation of the elect, it always—always, I say!—means only the true believers, since unbelievers have been excluded from that title as long as they are and remain unbelievers, nor can a different example be found anywhere.

Therefore, my inductive conclusion, which has been constructed from a sufficient enumeration [of causes], stands firm, and the truth prevails that the Scripture is completely unaware of that indiscriminate and unlimited election of all men equally, even of those who will never believe. Therefore, every time Huber distinguishes between a universal and an individual election[17], he commits the logical error of begging the ques-

---

15   *electione speciali*

16   *NEGO!*

17   *inter universalem et specialem electionem*

34

tion.[18] It falls to him to prove first that this combined predestination to salvation of both believers and unbelievers is taught anywhere in the Scriptures. Indeed, since so many things are taught in the Scriptures concerning election, predestination, the elect, the predestined, etc., it would be unthinkable that the Holy Spirit should have failed to teach clearly this universal election, and that He should have failed to declare all men to be elect, if what Dr. Huber so ardently contends were true.

We must go on to explore what else Huber weaves into his opinion. Indeed, the point of his argument about God's intention has been refuted abundantly above. That which he alleges concerning love has also been mentioned in an unfavorable light, but only in passing.

Now we are pleased to refute it expressly in this place.

Dr. Huber argues thus:

Election is just as general as love.

The love of God extends to the whole world, for "God so loved the world" (John 3).

Therefore, election, too, extends to the whole world.

We respond by making a distinction. The love of God is proclaimed in the Scriptures in two ways. One is general by which the entire human race was embraced by God in such a way that He sent His Son for the whole world, who made satisfaction for the sins of the entire world. But since, through and on account of unbelief, this love does not find a place among the largest part of the world, the result is that the election of the world does not arise out of that general love, especially since that love of God is not the entire cause of election. For Christ did

18   *peccat Elencho petitionis principii*

not say: "God so loved the world that He gave His only-begotten Son, that all men alike, whether they believe or whether they do not believe, are considered to be elect." Christ did not speak like this. Instead He said: "…so that everyone who *believes* in Him should not perish, but have eternal life."

But there is another love that is special—in the *Beloved*. This love is uniquely personal and belongs to the sons of God (Eph. 1). Faith is required for this love, as the Apostle testifies in Heb. 11: "It is impossible to please God without faith." Paul combines this love in the *Beloved* with the adoption as sons, just as John assigns the adoption only to those who receive Christ and believe in His name (John 1). In this individual love which is "in Christ Jesus our Lord" (Romans 8) or "in the *Beloved*" (Eph. 1), God embraces those whom He finds in the Beloved through faith. And this love for the elect children of God is not nullified, but carries all the way through to the end, just as it is written in John 13, "Since He loved *His own* who were in the world, He loved them *until the end*." Since this special love implies all the causes of election, namely, the charity of the Father; and Christ, in whom we were loved; then faith, by which alone we are pleasing to God in Christ. Therefore, this special love is of the same scope as election and pertains only to the truly believing. It cannot be denied that this distinction is founded on the Scriptures. For the testimonies that have already been produced confirm it beyond controversy, and Paul clearly teaches it in Romans 5. For he distinguishes, on the one hand, between the love of God with which He embraced us while we were still sinners and enemies, and that love, on the other hand, with which He embraces those who are justified and reconciled. He gives preference to this latter kind of love with which He now describes justified men as sons in a way that is incomparable with that other general form of love. "God," he says, "demonstrates His love toward us in that, when we were still sinners,

Christ died for us. Therefore, much more having been justified by His blood, we will be saved from wrath through Him. For if, when we were enemies, we were reconciled to God through the death of His Son, much more, having been reconciled, will we be saved from wrath through Him." Therefore, the chief role in establishing the definition and the efficacy of predestination to eternal life is assigned, not to that general form of love that extends even to Turks and to other unbelieving peoples, but to that narrower form of love that pertains to the children of God. Therefore, whenever Huber claims that we are denying that God loved the whole world, let it be understood that he is maliciously suppressing this aforementioned distinction of ours. But whenever he writes that God loves the whole world *in the Beloved*, then on those occasions let it be established without a doubt that he is manifestly doing injury to the apostolic text.

Another argument follows in which Dr. Huber seems especially to make his case.

All who are inscribed in the Book of Life are also elect.

All men are inscribed in the Book of Life.

Therefore, all are elect.

The major premise of this syllogism requires an explanation. But the minor premise is guilty of manifest falsehood. To the major premise we respond in this way, that it is a mistake with regard to phraseology. For not infrequently those also are said to be inscribed in the book of the living who, through the Sacrament of initiation [Baptism], are grafted into the Church, that is, the people of God, even as the saying is well-known and common: "We are inscribed in the Book of Life through Baptism and are brought back into the tablets of the covenant." This in-grafting, which takes place in time and, indeed, in the assembly of the Church, is clear enough on its own. But this temporal inscription into the Church Militant is not exactly the same as that other eternal inscription into the Church Triumphant which coincides with predestination or the election to eternal life. But as we have said, that in-grafting happens in time through Baptism and can again be abolished through impenitence, just as those who had been grafted into the olive tree of the people of God are again removed through unbelief (Rom. 11). Those who had been implanted into Christ through faith, if they begin to be unfruitful, are removed from Him, amputated and thrown out like useless branches that have been cut off (John 15). But when the expression is used with regard to that eternal inscription, it is certain that it refers to nothing other than God's gracious election, or the predestination to salvation. But if the major premise is understood in this sense, then the minor premise will immediately be recognized as notably false, affirming as it does that all men have been inscribed in the Book of Life by the eternal predestination of God.

But since Dr. Huber strives to prove this by means of various sayings of Scripture, let us see if his arguments carry any weight. First he offers the passage in Exodus 32 where Moses says to the Lord: "Either cause this punishment to depart from them, or if you will not, then blot me out of the book that you have written." To which the Lord responds: "The one who sins against Me—that one I will blot out of My book." Then that passage in Psalm 69: "Let them be blotted out of the book of the living, and let them not be written together with the righteous." Then the words of the Epistle to the Hebrews, chapter 12: "You have come near the assembly of the firstborn who have been written down in heaven, etc. See that you do not scorn Him who speaks, for if those who shunned him who spoke on the earth did not escape, much more will we not escape if we reject Him who is of heaven."

To the first we respond that the Lord rightly refuses to permit Moses to be blotted out, inasmuch as he who was truly one of the believing and elect was not worthy of being blotted out on account of a foreign sin perpetrated by the people. So when He says, "He who sins—this one I will blot out of My book," it is plain from Psalm 69 what it means to be blotted out of the Book of Life, namely, not to be written together with the righteous. For this is what the Psalmist says: "Let them be blotted out of the book of the living and let them not be written together with the righteous." There is, therefore, an *elenchus* of expression in the argument of Dr. Huber. Since the saying is metaphorical, it will not be in our power to interpret it freely as we wish, but we must rather heed the interpretation of the Holy Spirit. According to His interpretation, to be blotted out of the book of the living is the same thing as not to be inscribed. It is evident from Rev. 17 that this is the correct interpretation, where one reads about the reprobate men who (with regard to that eternal inscription and election of God) were never inscribed since the beginning of the world. "They will marvel," says John, "at the beast—the inhabitants of the earth whose names have not been written in the book of life since the *world was formed*." It has already been stated above what absurdities emerge from this "double" eternal inscription, that is, a "double" election and predestination[19].

Now, when the author of the Epistle to the Hebrews says, "You have come near to those who have been written down in heaven," he means those who, by faith in Jesus Christ, have been included among the faithful and elect—provided, of course, that they continue in the faith. For if they would not persevere in the good that has been begun, then they would not be among the elect, for although they might have been counted among the believers and the regenerated at one time, it was not in such a way

---

19   *electione et praedestinatione gemina*

that they could not fall again (Rom. 11).

Furthermore, in order that his general election might prevail, he also abuses the saying of the Apostle in Eph. 1: "He chose[20] us in Christ before the foundations of the world were laid." Huber says in Thesis 754: "For here Paul is speaking *universally* about *all* men. Absolutely no one was excluded from Christ in that decree of God, but all men have been included in the decree and in the Son, who is the Redeemer of the human race in common." He argues from Paul's saying in this way:

> All those whom Paul addresses with his epistle are embraced in the phrase, "He chose us in Him."

> Paul addresses the whole Church of the Ephesians without any distinction between believers and hypocrites.

> ***Therefore, they are all declared to be elected in Christ Jesus.***

We reply: Even if, for the most part, we were to concede the entire argument to him, nevertheless it would only deal with those who are called, and Huber would not yet have proven his primary thesis, which is that election also pertains to all people outside the assembly of the called, with no one (as he says) having been excluded. Therefore, this syllogism does not utter even a syllable about the peoples and men who have not been called.

Next, let Dr. Huber show us even one interpreter who, in expounding this Pauline epistle, has ever attempted to apply this conclusion to the entire[21] race of mortals.

---

20   *elegit*
21   *universum*

Thirdly, the Formula of Concord, in the article on predestination, mentions this very passage and most eloquently applies it only to the children of God, as we cited those words above.

Fourthly, the custom of the Holy Spirit has been noted, who is accustomed to addressing the visible assembly of the called and to speaking with titles of this kind that cannot be applied to every single individual in that assembly, but only to those who are true believers. Indeed, the synecdoche is common in the Scriptures in which that which applies to the more prominent part is attributed to the whole on account of that more prominent part. It is practically the same thing, then, when the whole field of grain is called "wheat," even though weeds, chaff, etc. are mixed in with it. This is how *Christ* Himself depicts the Church in the parables. Thus Luther explains[22], saying: "The Scripture commonly employs a figure of speech called the synecdoche, that is, it names something as a whole, understanding only some part of it. It does this, for example, with the people of Israel when it calls them the possession and the special people of God, even though the majority of them always belonged to the devil, while only a minority belonged to God. In the same way, Paul calls the Galatians, Corinthians, and other citizens 'the Churches of God,' even though only the smallest part of those citizens consisted of true children of God."

And certainly, if the things that Paul teaches in writing in this Epistle to the Ephesians pertain just as broadly and indiscriminately to all those who are called, even to the impenitent and profligate, it follows, then, that they, too, are incorporated in the Bride of Jesus Christ, regarding whom the Apostle proclaims in this very epistle that she has been sanctified, in such a way that she has no spot or blemish. But on the contrary, in chapter

22   Luther, *Against the Heavenly Prophets;* viz. *Luther's Works*, Vol. 40, p.197

5, Paul distinctly separates the profligate from the benefits of the children of God. "You know," he says, "that no fornicator or impure or greedy person has any inheritance in the kingdom of Christ and of God."

Indeed, does not the very structure of the words refute Huber's violent interpretation? Paul writes "to the *saints*, who are in Ephesus, and to the faithful in Christ Jesus." Concerning these he then adds: "He has blessed us with every spiritual blessing in the heavenly realms in Christ." But it is those who are *of faith* who are blessed with the believing Abraham" (Gal. 3). Therefore, those who are not of faith are not numbered among the blessed. Why? Because, whenever he writes about those whose election was made in Christ, Paul is speaking about these very people who are blessed and elected to the kingdom of God, whom the Savior also addresses thus: "Come, you blessed by My Father, inherit the kingdom prepared for you *since the beginning of the world.*" And yet, the impenitent are not in Christ, but outside of Him, because they are without faith. How, then, can he accommodate that apostolic preaching regarding the elect to those who are impure, unbelieving and impenitent? From these things, all those who take the orthodox truth of the divine Word to heart can clearly see how far removed the Apostle Paul is from defending Dr. Huber.

Let us also refute the Huberian argument concerning Judas, whom Dr. Huber also declares to have been elected at some time, since it is written, "I have guarded those whom You gave Me, and none of them is lost except for that son of perdition." From this Dr. Huber gathers that Judas also had been given to Christ, that is, elected to eternal life. We respond that never before has any theologian dared to interpret in this way or to twist the Savior's saying so that He declares Judas to have been ascribed to the elect children of God. For Christ protests loudly against this jarring interpretation, saying to the Apostles in John 13: "If you know these things, you are blessed if you do them. I am not speaking about all of you. I know *those whom* I have chosen," undoubtedly excluding Judas the betrayer from those whom He has chosen. In fact, in that very chapter from which Dr. Huber draws these things, this violent interpretation of his is refuted. The Savior says: "I have manifested Your name to the men whom You gave Me from *the world*." Likewise, "I do not pray for the world, but for those whom *You gave* Me." Since, with these words, a distinction is clearly being made between those who were given *to Christ* on the one hand, and the world on the other, we beg Huber to explain to us whether he ascribes Judas to the world, or to those who were given to Christ out of the world? We definitely state that he is to be classified with the world. Therefore, he must have been separated from those who were given *to Christ* out of the *world*, by way of eternal election. Meanwhile, we are not unwilling to grant that Judas, together with the other Eleven, was elected to the Apostolate, since the Lord says in John 5: "Have I not chosen you twelve? And yet one of you is a devil." Indeed, Christ had a certain regard for this personal benefit in this prayer of His. For He separates the Apostles themselves from those who would believe through their preaching. Therefore, with that election to the Apostolate in view, He says that none of them (that is, none of the Apostles) had been lost, "except for the son of perdition." But if these things should be extended beyond the order of the Apostles to the company of all men, then a most absurd interpretation arises from this, as if no one from the entire human race (which was elected as a whole to eternal life) should perish except for Judas alone. No one needs our admonitions to understand how monstrously false this is.

He cites a saying of Christ from the same chapter: "You gave Him authority over all flesh." Huber says that this means that all human flesh has been elected and predestined to eternal life. But if someone is of the opinion that this "giving authority over all flesh" must refer entirely to predestination, then the sense of this phrase ("over all flesh") must be the same as the sense in Joel 2, "I will pour out My Spirit on all flesh," which would be absolutely unsuitable to apply to all individuals of the human race. For by this reasoning, this prophecy would never have been fulfilled, because the Holy Spirit was never given nor will He be given to all men in common. But just the same, authority has been given to Christ over all flesh, for by the acquired universal merit for the propitiation of the entire human race, authority has been granted to Him over all people, either for salvation in the case of believers, or for judgment in the case of those who despise this obtained benefit of Christ. And for this reason, when the Savior refers to salvation, He adds a restriction, saying: "That He may give eternal life to *as many as You gave Him*." Hence we make the following argument:

As many (by way of eternal predestination) as were given to Christ by the Father, to these eternal life is given.

Eternal life is given to believers.

Therefore, only believers were given to Christ by the Father by way of eternal election.

The major premise belongs to Christ Himself in the words that have been cited. The minor premise likewise belongs to Christ, that is, that eternal life is given only to believers. Consequently, He immediately adds: "And this is eternal life, that *they may know* You, the only true God, and the one whom You sent, Jesus Christ." From this it follows that only believers and those who know God and Christ have been predestined and elected to life.

The objection is also made by some people: Even though we teach that all men are not elected broadly and indiscriminately whether they believe or not, couldn't the doctrine of the Calvinists be more easily refuted if we taught an election that is universal and extends to all men? But we respond: There is no need for us to resort to a lie in order to bolster the truth, just as the Holy Spirit does not need to use fantasies to teach the Word of God, as Syracides[23] says, nor does He need to use false hypotheses in order to refute His adversaries. The truth stands all by itself.[24] For, on the one hand, we teach that God does not absolutely desire the death of any man, but seriously desires that all men be saved. We build this argument on the foundations of Holy Scripture. On the other hand, it is certain that not all are now saved, but according to the sentence of Christ, although many are called, few are found to be elect. All the fault for men's destruction lies, not in some will of God, as the Calvinists wickedly teach, but completely and entirely in men themselves, since not only do they not believe, but they do not even want to make use of the means (through which the Holy Spirit would have worked faith in them). This has been broadly, sufficiently, and thoroughly treated in an orthodox manner in the theses.

Besides, if we were to take up a false hypothesis in order to refute the Calvinists, by pretending that God elected all men to salvation, even those who never have believed nor will believe in Jesus Christ, we cannot tell which ruin would be worse. For in pretending one error, we would fall into another error on the opposite extreme—much like Illyricus[25] thought that he could refute once and for all the synergism of the human will if he contended that the very essence of our nature is sin.

23   Ecclesiasticus (Sirach) in the Apocrypha. An allusion to chapter 34 of that book.
24   *Ipsa per se sibi constat veritas.*
25   A reference to the heresy of Matthias Flacius Illyricus (1520–1575), which is condemned in the first article of the Formula of Concord.

Another argument

But Dr. Huber objects, saying that, according to our conclusion, none were elected before believing; likewise, that election, as described by us, is preceded by the faith of men. Indeed,
in this area he does us a genuine injustice. For we state that election was made in eternity itself, before the foundations of the
world were laid (Eph. 1); but we state that faith is kindled in us
in time.

How can it be claimed, then, that we state that something
that is effected in time precedes or comes before something that
takes place in eternity? But the reason for this lies in Huber's
hallucination, for he does not consider carefully enough that
God elected them according to His foreknowledge in eternity,
whence He knew ahead of time that salvation would come about
by means of the merit of Christ the Redeemer, apprehended by
faith.[26] Certainly the Mömpelgard Colloquy[27] does not hesitate
to call faith a cause of election. But whether it is called a cause
or a limitation or an infallible sign of the elect, it is clear that no
one was predestined to salvation apart from any consideration of
faith whatsoever[28] (insofar as it lays hold of Christ). Indeed, in
physical or natural matters, a cause is always either prior to its
effect in time, or at the same time as its effect, while being prior
to it in logical order. It works differently in matters of the will[29],
where the effect can be fixed in view of something that is still to
come with regard to time.

---

26   *quo praescivit, Christi Redemptoris merito fide apprehenso salva-
tum iri*
27   This Colloquy between Lutheran and Calvinist theologians took
place March 14–27, 1586. The resulting conflict over the doctrine of the
Calvinists which was set forth at Mömpelgard regarding Predestination was
what caused Huber to lose his standing among the Calvinists.
28   *Absque ullo prorsus intuitu fidei*
29   *Secus res habet in voluntariis*

We are pleased to prove the matter with another example: The sending of the Son into the world and His suffering are, with regard to time, after our predestination (since predestination was done from eternity, and the sending and suffering of Christ took place at the consummation of the ages – Heb. 9). And yet Huber cannot deny that this sending into the world and suffering of the Lord is the cause because of which we were predestined to salvation. I would also like Dr. Huber to weigh this carefully, that two things can be mutual causes, but in a different class of causes. How? In that our faith was never in the future for God, but was entirely present outside the realm of time, inasmuch as to Him nothing is either past or future, but all things are entirely present at the same time, in such a way that precisely when speaking about the eternal predestination of God, He actually destines believers to life rather than *predestining* those who would believe.

Huber frequently also sets this reheated cabbage before us and places particular hope of victory in it:

If God, in electing men, passes over no one, then He certainly elects all.

God passes over no one in His election.

Therefore, He elected each and every man.

We reply: The minor premise is false. Indeed, with His antecedent will, which is mercy, He passes over no one, but desires that all men be saved. But with His consequent will, which takes into account[30] the unbelief of men, He passes over those whom He sees will persevere in unbelief, and for this very reason, He does not elect them. Certainly Christ Himself, in saying that "few are chosen,"[31] teaches that the rest were passed over,

---

30   *respicit*
31   *electos*

but not with an absolute hatred, as the Calvinists want to believe, but because of foreseen final impenitence. Therefore, Huber always stumbles over this stone, because he asserts that election is to be defined only by that antecedent will of God, thus confusing cause and effect. For that beneficent and merciful will of God is the cause of election, but not the solitary cause, not the whole[32] cause, as we have demonstrated above.

But Huber goes on:

If God passed over some, then He passed them over by absolute decree.

This latter is absurd.

Therefore, the former also is absurd.

Now, the major premise is roundly denied. For although He passed over in His election those whom He saw would persevere until the end in impenitence, He did not pass them over by an absolute decree or in hatred, but on account of that very final impenitence and unbelief of theirs. Nor does this unbelief depend on that passing over of God, as an effect depends on a cause (as Huber falsely imagines), but rather the foreseen unbelief causes that passing over. For those who were not going to believe—and that, by their own fault—would, naturally, also neglect the instrument of faith and the means of eternal salvation. And God, who beholds all this in the present, foreknew this in eternity—that they would persevere in unbelief—and so He did not deem them fit for His election. Therefore, it was not right that Huber should have hurled the charge at us of teaching an absolute election. Not we, but he, clings to this charge, that there was some sort of absolute election of all men together, and dreaming that it was not bounded with any regard for faith in

---

32   ὁλική

Christ,[33] inasmuch as He caused it to stretch out even over those who would never be gifted with any faith in God or in *Christ*, nor would they believe at any time in the future.

But, dear reader, observe how unskillfully Huber fights against us from that little garrison of "passing over," to which he objects, since not even he (to the highest degree possible he descends from his invented general election to the special and true election that separates the sheep from the goats, the elect from the reprobate, those who are to be saved from those who are to be damned) can deny that this election, which separates the elect from the damned, necessarily implies a view of faith and its opposite, unbelief, inasmuch as God elects believers and passes over unbelievers. But surely he does not also now concede that he is straying into an absolute decree, as he accuses us of doing?

If he roars that he, however, presupposes a universal election, and for that reason is not falling headlong into an absolute decree, we will respond that we, too, presuppose a universal *will of God*, of which we have spoken, which Huber improperly keeps referring to as universal election. And yet, while he insists that he is speaking about election properly so called, he permits a contradiction, for by the very etymological and grammatical meaning of the verb ("to elect") which is proven by the authority of Moses and of Christ, he is irrefutably defeated, as was demonstrated above.

Let us hear Huber's reasoning again: If not all were elected, then those who were not elected were also never able to believe or to make a beginning of faith, because they would not have anything to believe. Therefore, in order that they may be able to believe, he thinks that the dogma of some universal predestination and election of all men to eternal life—even of those who would never believe—must be set before them. Otherwise,

33   *nulloque fidei in Christum respectu limitatam somnians*

they must always be hesitant, wondering whether election also pertains to them. This hesitation must pose an obstacle to them, for which reason they are less capable of conceiving faith.

We respond: If we had concluded that some were passed over and excluded from election by an absolute will of God, then such an objection would surely militate against our position. But now what need is there for that preposterous anxiety, since God wants to exclude no one from the election of His grace except for those very ones who exclude themselves through impenitence or final unbelief?

In addition, Dr. Huber wants everyone to establish his own election *a priori*, to peek first into the book of life, and, if he sees that all men without distinction are written together in it—Jews and Turks and Tartarus and Cannibals and other damned men—then, finally, he should conceive faith that election pertains to him, too. Thus Huber wants the faith of men to be built on the foundation of such an election that also includes the reprobate, the Jews and the Turks, that is, all unbelieving peoples, and that can be rendered useless, changed and voided. Oh, splendid reasoning by which faith is to be confirmed!

But the foundation of our election stands firm, having this seal: "The Lord knows those who are His." Indeed, we have other hypotheses on which a man can meditate and thus come to faith, by the power of the Holy Spirit, namely, the universal promises of the Gospel, that God wants all men to be saved. Therefore, if someone inquires, "Does God perhaps not want me to believe?," I reply, "On the contrary, God truly desires not only that you be saved, but that you also believe and come to a knowledge of the truth (1 Tim. 2). In fact, He even provides you with the instrument[34] of salvation, which He wants you to use whenever you are unable to kindle faith in yourself. Hear

34 *organa*

50

the Word, through which God wishes to be efficacious." We set forth this will of God revealed in the Word as the foundation. As we expressed above, Dr. Huber calls this will of God "universal election," but only by weaving in a contradiction.

Let us examine the rest of Huber's arguments.

Among other things, he draws this conclusion: "Those who deduce the particulary election[35] from God's foreknowledge[36] are not very different from the Calvinists, who construct it out of God's will[37]." Therefore, since Dr. Huber's colleagues deduce a particular election from God's foreknowing, Huber then concludes that his colleagues do not differ greatly from the Calvinians.

We respond: "Woe to you, most blessed Apostle Paul! For you yourself deduced from God's foreknowledge your conclusion about that predestination that you assign only to the justified and to those who are to be glorified in the blessedness of life, saying: 'Those whom He foreknew'—pay attention, Huber!— 'Those whom He foreknew, He predestined' (Rom. 8)." St. Peter agrees with this, calling the believers "those who were elected according to the *foreknowledge* of God the Father" (1 Pet. 1).

Now, surely these Apostles are not also to be considered as favoring the Calvinistic decree of an absolute predestination, are they? In addition, when the Calvinians ascribe the destruction of reprobate men to God's *foreknowledge*, everyone understands that this *will* of God (and even an absolute will) openly opposes the revealed will, and ends up being a cause of men's perdition. In turn, when we teach with the Apostle that God pre-

35   *particulariam electionem*; the proper Latin phrase (*particularem electionem*) is used below. A marginal note reads: *He calls it "particulary"* (*particulariam*), *using bad Latin out of spite.*
36   *ex praescire Dei*
37   *ex velle Dei*

destined those whom He foreknew (that is, those who would continually believe in the world's Savior) to salvation, while the rest, whom God saw would never believe in Him or would abandon the faith again, were disregarded for this very reason, here the *foreknowledge* itself does not include the cause, but rather the acquaintance with it. But the thing that is foreseen, namely, faith in Jesus Christ, is either a limitation or (by reason of being included in its correlative, namely, Christ) a cause of election, as the Mömpelgard Colloquy calls it, just as also the foreseen unbelief is a true cause why the reprobate are disregarded and damned. For just as in the revealed Word of the Gospel, God reveals how He saves or damns men, so He proposed from eternity in what way He elects to salvation, or leaves behind in damnation. But the Word reveals that he who believes is not judged, but is saved; but that he who does not believe is judged already, because he does not believe in the name of God's only-begotten Son (John 3). Therefore God so established this very thing also in eternity; He so decreed that He wanted to save those who would believe and damn those who would not believe. For the word of the Gospel is nothing other than the manifestation of that very eternal purpose of God, as Paul testifies in Rom. 16, Eph. 5, 2 Tim. 1.

Huber objects that what the Apostle says ("Those whom He foreknew" – Rom. 8) applies equally to all men. Therefore he ridiculously insults us, saying that we are breaking off this link of the Pauline chain by citing his words. **We respond**: We can offer innumerable citations of orthodox theologians in which not all the links are always expressly mentioned one by one in mentioning this Pauline chain in Rom. 8, but neither are they for that reason broken off. Rather, they are implicitly included. Then let Dr. Huber show us any theologian who has ever dared to affirm that this passage in Rom. 8 applies equally to all men. The context argues that the message there is being delivered about those *who love God*, who are made *in conformity* with the likeness of God's Son; who, having been foreseen, are predestined; who, having been predestined, are called; who, having been called, are justified; and who, having been justified, are finally glorified. Fully mindful and aware of this, Huber extends this link of the apostolic chain ("whom He foreknew") over good and evil at the same time through the passage of his universal election, in which even those are imagined to have been predestined who never love God, who are not made in conformity with the likeness of the Son of God, who are neither foreknown as those who would be in Christ by faith, nor are they justified—regardless of how much they were called, nor are they finally glorified.

He accomplishes nothing at all by throwing the Book of Concord at us. As a matter of fact, the Book of Concord distinguishes between the predestination and the foreknowledge of God when it says plainly: "The foreknowledge or foresight of God, with which He foresees and foreknows all things before they come to be, extends over all creatures, both evil and good. For the Lord knows ahead of time by this foresight or foreknowledge, and He sees everything that is or will ever be, etc."[38] Therefore, *Concordia* speaks about the limitless "present tense" of God, under the umbrella of which even the devils are contained, and indeed, all creatures. For God foreknew what even the devils would do. If Huber thinks that the passage of the Apostle ("Those whom He foreknew, He also predestined") should be taken in this unbounded meaning that extends over all creatures, it follows, then, that not only all men, but also the devils, and, for that matter, all creatures, were predestined to eternal life! These things irrefutably demonstrate how much violence Huber does to Holy Scripture with his contorted explanations, and how fragile is the foundation on which he builds the structure of his opinion.

---

38   Formula: SD: XI:4

But let us proceed to other arguments of Huber that must be aired out. He thinks that, with our predestination in which we teach that only those were elected by God whom He foreknew as persevering in faith until the end, such uncertainty is attached that no one can comprehend or include either himself or anyone else in the benefit of election. Indeed, Huber thinks that the whole election, as we teach it, pertains properly to the dead and not to the living. **I respond**: What is this we hear? Can it be that Huber is actually striving to reintroduce the papistic errors that were once removed and banned from the churches of their lands? We do not build the certainty of salvation on the article on election in this way. God Himself, in the eternal purpose of election, immutably states that He earnestly wants to save ***all men***—all who believe in Christ Jesus and persevere continually until the end. Now, I believe in Christ, and I know that God will preserve me in the faith continually until the end. Therefore, I am certainly one of the elect. If Huber wants to deny that which is here assumed, namely, that a Christian can know whether or not he believes and whether or not he will persevere continually until the end with the help of God, then let him go over to the papists as one who approves with them the canon of the Council of Trent that says that no one can be certain of his continual perseverance until the end (Canon 16). Let us recall the very canon of the Council of Trent that says this: "If anyone says with absolute and infallible certainty that he considers himself to have that great gift of continual perseverance until the end, unless he learns it by special revelation, let him be anathema."

Therefore it should now be evident to Huber that he is waging war against the Evangelical Churches—indeed, against the Apostles themselves, who also most clearly declare that Christians, even in this life, can be certain of their faith and of their perseverance in the faith. For ***Christ*** promises this to His sheep, that no one can snatch them out of His and the Father's hands. To be sure, any true Christian can draw the following conclusion: I am a little sheep *of Christ*. Therefore, no one will ever be able to snatch me from the hands of *Christ* the Shepherd. Paul builds the certainty of his salvation on this foundation: "I know and am certain that He in whom I have believed is able to guard my deposit continually until that day." Indeed, he is not writing about himself only, but about all those who love God: "I know that neither death nor life, neither angels nor principalities nor authorities, neither the present nor the future, neither height nor depth can separate us from the love of *God* that is in *Christ Jesus* our Lord" (Romans 8). And 2 The. 3: "Not everyone has faith. But God is faithful, and He will make you steadfast and will preserve you from evil." St. Peter confirms this in 1 Peter 1, declaring that the elect are "guarded by faith in the power of *God* for salvation." He then repeats it in chapter 5. So then, unless Huber wishes to pin a note of uncertainty onto these sacrosanct promises, it must be plainly confessed that believers are able even in this life, not only to be certain for themselves of their faith—just as it says in 2 Cor. 13 ("Prove yourselves, whether you are in the faith")—but also to be certain of their perseverance in the faith, and that, not only after death, as Huber writes constantly along the lines of the papists, but even now in this life.

Neither conscience nor duty will permit us here to remain silent. We cannot fail to warn the Church of God about the slander with which Dr. Huber shamelessly misrepresents us, his colleagues, against the testimony of both his heart and his conscience, as if we were stating that "before the final perseverance" (these are his words) "there is no election of men with God." He charges us with this most daringly in his latest writing that has been scattered among the studious. He has entitled it, *Samuel Huber's Confession of Election*, and he directs his arguments—especially the seventh one—against this concept.

Against this slander we solemnly protest that an appalling charge is being leveled against us by Huber. We have testified many times that our election was made *in eternity*, and that, before the foundations of the world were laid, all those were elected whom God *foreknew* according to His foreknowledge (as Peter and Paul affirm) that they would be constantly incorporated in Christ Jesus, and would be saved through faith in Christ Jesus. We have also taught over and over again that a man can, even before his death, be certain of his perseverance in the faith and thus also of his election *from eternity*, which has been proven just now with infallible words and promises of the Scriptures.

Chapter II: Concerning Justification

Our Churches have always taught and still teach the justification that is by faith and that pertains to believers, but that by no means extends to the whole world.

Besides this justification by faith, Dr. Huber teaches some other justification that is equally common to the entire human race. Indeed, writing against Kimedontius,[39] he says on page 245:"All those to whom the Gospel goes out are called elect, and likewise justified, sanctified, redeemed." Page 19 against Kimedontius: "Huber condemns as Sarracenic language to say that nothing is more contrary to the Pauline doctrine than to imagine that justification extends as generally and widely as the condemnation is general and extends equally to all and over all men[40]." Since Dr. Huber condemns this proposition here in this place, it clearly means that he teaches a justification that does apply to all mortals. Hence he writes in his *Tübingen Theses*, Thesis 270: "Moreover, this status and condition belongs to our redemption, by which sins have been forgiven to all men equally, since the handwriting that was against us has been blotted out (Col. 2). But in that general **remission of sins** that came upon us through the blood of Christ, many are included who are ungrateful to God, and so they try to destroy and scatter the family by the wickedness of their life. Because of this, although they **received** the remission of sins, nevertheless, on account of their negligence, they are **again** condemned, and are compelled to repay all their debts."[41] Theses 59 and 60: "But meanwhile, no

---

39   Jakob Kimedontius (1550–1596), a Reformed theologian who wrote on the topic of Predestination.

40   *In omnes et super omnes*

41   The original thesis continues: "Nothing can be said more clearly concerning the reprobate: We understand that they were saved through Christ

less truly, properly, actually and effectively has Christ conferred redemption on the entire human race—just as truly, properly, actually and effectively as Adam brought ruin upon each and every man. And lest anything remain in doubt, we are saying that, by the death and satisfaction of Christ for our sins, all judgment and divine wrath upon all men has been rightly, truly and properly removed and blotted out."[42] Thesis 62: "This (Sacramentarian) spirit should not bellow so loudly. And yet, everyone understands that this is the very thing that he rages about. He claims that it is not **properly** to be understood that the Scripture says that Christ truly washed away all of Adam's guilt in all men. For no less truly and **properly** did He wash it away than Adam truly and properly brought sin and death on his entire race." In Thesis 65, he writes: "The heavenly Father accepted the death of

just as much as anyone else was. But, if they return to their vomit, the grace of God is abolished in them and Christ is made to no avail, and thus they perish by the fresh guilt of their disobedience."

42   Huber's entire Thesis 59 reads: "Thus also Christ is the catholic Redeemer who has freed all people from all sin and takes away all the sin that came into the world through Adam. But at the same time, the fact that some still perish is not to be reckoned to a lack of redemption, nor on account of them should Christ be denied as the universal Redeemer of the human race. To be sure, those who perish do so by their own vice and by the deception of Satan, to whom they again subject themselves. But meanwhile, no less truly, properly, actually and effectively has Christ conferred redemption on the entire human race—just as truly, properly, actually and effectively as Adam brought ruin upon each and every man." Thesis 60: "And lest anything remain in doubt, we are saying that, by the death and satisfaction of Christ for our sins, all judgment and divine wrath upon all men has been rightly, truly and properly removed and blotted out. Indeed, God established this very thing and sent His Son for this very purpose. And so we affirm that God was truly and undoubtedly reconciled with the entire human race by the death of Christ, by a better ransom." Thesis 61: "With regard to what Grynaeus has in his Theses about which we have spoken above—that Christ cannot properly be said to have suffered for those who perish, or, in other words, for the entire human race, we say that this is the same as if he said that Christ did not properly do what the Scriptures say He did, which we interpret to mean that the Scriptures attribute to Christ things that are most false and deceptive."

Christ, so that through it, truly and undoubtedly all men were at once freed from all sin and condemnation, on account of which also, in that very act, the entire human race was received into His grace and bosom." He explains what this means at greater length in his book against Kimedontius, where, on page 246, he calls it a "general adoption." And then he writes on pages 247 and 248: "All of us are loved in the Son, just as Christ says in John 3: 'God so loved the world, that He gave His only-begotten Son.' To be loved in the Son is nothing other than to be received into the embrace of **God**, and that all wrath is taken away, just as John also says in 1 John 4: 'He loved us and sent His Son as the propitiation for our sins.' And thus Paul also says that from the very beginning, **all men** to whom he preaches the Gospel of Christ Jesus are called ἠγαπημένους and beloved, Ephesians 1."

In Thesis 157 he writes: "For God loved all men in His Beloved, just as Paul also says when he brings all nations (with no man among all nations being excepted) back under that **eternal embrace**[43] of divine grace (Eph. 1 and 3, Rom. 16, Gal. 1). Until now we have heard many arguments, and especially these, that the kingdom of grace extends over the whole world."[44]

From these and many other examples from his own published books and writings, we are unable to come to any other conclusion but that Dr. Huber is clearly persuaded that, at some time (whether in eternity, or when God made the first promise in Paradise, or when Christ was sacrificed on the altar of the cross), the entire human race was—*was*, I say!—for the sake of the merit of Christ, truly received into grace, into the bosom and embrace of God; and that all men were loved in the Beloved through some general adoption; and that, through a justification that is just as general and extends just as widely as the condem-

---

43   *sub istum ab aeterno complexum gratiae divinae*
44   Marginal note: "And here I thought that the kingdom of grace was properly the Church of God."

nation from Adam extends widely upon all men equally, sins were forgiven to all men equally through a general remission of sins[45]; redemption was conferred on the entire human race in that very act and deed; and Adam's guilt has been truly and properly washed away in all men, so much so that all judgment and wrath of God has been removed and blotted out in all men—truly and properly. These are Huber's own words, faithfully transcribed from his books.

Here one may ask Dr. Huber when he thinks all this took place. When were all sins remitted equally to the entire human race? He has to confess one or the other—that this took place either from eternity, or in time. But it will be clearly demonstrated shortly that neither of these options can be true. We interpret those things that the Scripture contains regarding the redemption and reconciliation of the world[46] (or of the human race) concerning the benefit gained and acquired through the death of Christ, and concerning the sufficiency of that merit of Christ—that it is sufficient for the whole world to be reconciled, justified and saved, if the whole world were to believe; that it was also intended for the world and acquired to this end, that all men should thence obtain salvation through faith. Meanwhile, God has never intended it to mean that it avails for justifying or for remitting sins without faith, through some sort of general remission of sins or justification, which is also supposedly done among those who never have faith, never had faith, or never will have faith. He who does not believe, says John the Baptist, will not see life, but the wrath of God remains on him (John 3). Therefore, regarding those who never believe in the Son of God, from them also the wrath of God was never withdrawn (not even for a moment). However much the treasure of the expiation of sins has been ob-

---

45 Marginal note: "So dreams Dr. Huber."
46 Marginal note: "How the sayings regarding redemption and reconciliation are to be understood."

tained for them and offered to them in the Gospel, nevertheless, it was never conferred on them through unbelief, nor was it ever received by them, since faith was lacking to them, which is the only organ for receiving the remission of sins.

And how inconsistent it is to state such a thing is rendered plain from the assigned distribution. If Dr. Huber should say that sins were remitted to the entire world from eternity, and that all men were justified, and that this general remission of the sins of all men is then abolished for the reprobate in time, then let him respond clearly how it is abolished for them, and when. If they are conceived through original sin, when they are, to be sure, in an original state of wickedness, what kind of grace is this, then, that is supposed to justify those who do not exist, so that as soon as they begin to exist, they are absorbed into their prior condemnation, and all of that which was granted to them in eternity, while they still didn't exist, vanishes into nothingness?

Indeed, how could original sin be remitted to them from eternity, if it is imputed to them for condemnation in time? Or if it be the case that original sin was truly and properly remitted to them by some remission that took place before they came to be, it follows, then, that they are born justified; they are born sons, not of wrath, but of grace; they are born saints, to whom original sin cannot be injurious, inasmuch as it was remitted to them and forgiven by that general forgiveness. What, then, remains of the declaration of Christ, "Truly, truly I tell you, unless a man is born again of water and the Spirit, he cannot enter the kingdom of heaven. What is born of flesh is flesh" (John 3)? It should follow that, in addition, believers are now righteous before God through a double justification[47], one that is general, without faith; another that is individual, through faith. Yet why is there any need for justification by faith, if even without faith

---

47   *gemina justificatione*

this remission of sins and the grace of God are conferred?

In addition, since this general justification, according to Dr. Huber's hypothesis, embraces also unbelievers, let him respond to this: Were sins forgiven to them through the imputation of the obedience of Christ, or apart from it? If it was without the imputation of the obedience of Christ, then the eternal justice of God will be endangered, since He remits sins without regard for a mediating satisfaction. But if it is through the imputation of the merit of Christ, then let him explain: Does the Scripture ever, anywhere, mention any bare, simple imputation that is considered without respect to faith? And what need is there for several, since the Apostle teaches one method and one way alone for obtaining remission of sins, and that is through faith, so that he exclaims that, "We are not justified *except* through faith in Jesus Christ" (Gal. 2). There are a great many sermons on the justification of men before God in our published writings—in the Augsburg Confession, the Apology, the Smalcald Articles, in both Catechisms of Luther, in the Epitome and the Formula of Concord—indeed, in the entire controversy with the papists that has gone on now for more than 70 years. But regarding this general justification by which all men were supposedly justified at some time, received into the embrace of divine grace, adopted, with sin having been forgiven to all men equally—truly, properly and by the deed itself—of this, I say, in all of these published writings and in all of Holy Scripture, there is nothing but eternal silence.

For when it says in Romans 5, "Just as through the sin of one man, evil spread to all men for condemnation, so through the righteousness of one man, good spreads to all men for justification of life,"[48] this is clearly what Paul means, that just as

48   *Sicut per unius delictum propagatum est malum in omnes homines ad condemnationem, ita per unius propagationem iustificatur bonum in omnes homines ad justificationem vitae.* Note several differences from the

through the transgression of Adam, sin spread to all those who came after him resulting in their condemnation, so through the obedience of Christ, righteousness was acquired and obtained, which is more than sufficient for all men to be justified and made alive, if the whole world were to embrace it by faith. For this is how Romans 3 explains this sentence: "The righteousness of God through faith in Jesus Christ *to all and upon all those who believe.*" One should not look to the Huberian dogma in order to confirm the true sense of the Pauline saying. For it is true that the Apostle, in each passage, mentions the established antithesis of propagation between Adam and Christ, not only of evil for condemnation, but also of good for justification. Now, certainly, if one should press each and every aspect of the antithesis, wouldn't we fall into the heresy of the papists, so that, just as sin was propagated from Adam to men through the indwelling of sin, so the righteousness of the Second Adam likewise must be transmitted and propagated to us by way of indwelling? But if we condemn this mode of propagation of the one[49], then it follows that no other mode exists for propagating in us the righteousness that avails before God, except for imputation. For salvation and the righteousness obtained for the whole world are apprehended through faith, so that those who believe apply that to themselves which would have been propagated through imputation by faith to all men, if all men had believed.

Therefore, although on account of a lack of faith, all men at once are by no means justified, nor were they ever justified, nevertheless the apostolic antithesis remains unshaken. Nor is

Vulgate and the grammatical inconsistencies in the second half of the sentence. Literal translation: "...so through the propagation of one man, good is justified in all men for justification of life." Perhaps a typographic error inverting *propagationem* and *justificatur.* Suggested reading as rendered above: "*...ita per unius justitiam propagatur bonum...*"

49   The Book of Concord rejects the notion that man is justified by the indwelling righteousness of Christ. Formula: SD, art. iii, par. 54.

the good or the benefit that is conferred on us through Christ rendered weaker than the evil that was transmitted to us by Adam's sin. For Christ surpasses Adam in this, that, since through *one* sin death reigned, Christ, for His part, obtained full justification from *many* sins for all those who believe in His name.

He also surpasses Adam in this, that Adam killed those who came after him, that is, he delivered death and condemnation to them by the propagation of sin. Christ, however, brings us back from condemnation to justification of life. Now, just as it is a much greater work to bring to life one who is by nature dead than it is to kill someone (since anyone can kill, while no one is able to bring to life except for God, with His omnipotent power), so also Christ is to be regarded as having surpassed Adam by bringing to life those whom Adam, through sin, had made subject to death.

And if Dr. Huber were teachable, the learned and vigorous response of the Wittenberg theologians could have abundantly satisfied him. This is how they respond to Huber regarding that passage championed by Huber, Romans 5: "On the contrary, isn't your conclusion manifestly overthrown by that very passage that you cite, clearly demonstrating that there is no valid reason for your opposition? To be sure, just as the condemnation pertained to all men *by guilt*[50], and nevertheless *actually*[51] pertains only to the impenitent and unbelieving, so also the gift of the grace of God and the merit of Christ is certainly universal. Nevertheless, it is actually restricted to believers only—those who are released from condemnation by the benefit of Christ, who is apprehended by faith." Thus far the Wittenberg theologians.

And what will Dr. Huber reply to the Book of Concord, which, in citing these very words from Romans, explicitly con-

---

50   *reatu*
51   *actu*

firms that those things mean nothing other than that we are justified by faith? This is what the Book of Concord says in the Latin edition, page 666: "Therefore, these statements are equivalent and clearly mean the same thing, when Paul says that we are *justified by faith*; or that *faith is imputed to us for righteousness;* and when he teaches that we are *justified by the obedience of one Mediator, who is Christ*; or that *through the righteousness of one man, justification of life comes upon all men*. For faith does not justify on account of this, that it is such a good work, or that it is such a splendid virtue, but because it apprehends and embraces the merit of **Christ** in the promise of the Gospel." Thus far the Book of Concord[52].

If the Pauline phrase (that "through the righteousness of one Man, justification of life comes upon all men") clearly means the same thing as that other statement, "We are justified by faith" (as the Book of Concord clearly and emphatically asserts), then the interpretation is rejected by the sentence of the Book of Concord that imagines from these words of Paul a justification apart from faith—one that extends also to those who have never had faith and never will. Dr. Luther says it even better in [his lectures on] the second chapter to the Galatians: "Where Christ and *faith* are not present, there is *no* remission of sins, no refuge, nothing but pure imputation of sins and condemnation."[53]

---

52   Formula:SD:III: 12-13
53   This quotation of Luther can be found in Luther's works in English, Volume 26, Page 133, treating Galatians 2:16.

Chapter III: Concerning Regeneration

Concerning regeneration in the article of Baptism, Dr. Huber dissents from us no less than in the former matters. In the question of whether all those who are baptized in infancy are regenerated by means of that Baptism, there is no difference of opinion among us. But when the question is asked concerning adults, we teach that not all adults are alike regenerated when they seek and receive Baptism at an adult age, since it is possible that someone may undergo Baptism with a dishonest, hypocritical, wicked, and impenitent heart, just as many of the Jews or wandering Egyptians[54] receive Baptism only for the sake of gaining property rights, pretending meanwhile that they desire the Sacrament of Baptism with a sense of true godliness. We contend that people such as these receive a valid[55] Baptism in regard to essence, but, while regeneration itself is offered to them, it is not conferred on them, nor is it received by them.

Instead, Dr. Huber states that regeneration occurs with all those who are properly baptized[56], even those adults who are baptized in their impenitence, so that, in his words:

The work of God is this: *Regeneration and reception into grace* are complete, although its benefit and fruit do not come upon anyone unless they are claimed and applied by faith. Indeed, no exceptions are to be made here in the case of adults, since the passages in Romans 6 and Galatians 3 teach that all people without equivocation are said to have been baptized into the death of Christ, and are said to be clothed with Christ—as many as were

---

54   *errones Aegyptii*
55   *integrum*
56   *rite baptizatis*

baptized. If we allow an exception to this, then the Calvinists will also be allowed to make exceptions and press their equivocations.

Regeneration is necessarily **conferred** in the act of Baptism, whether adults apply themselves to the work and institution of God by faith or whether they do not, that is, whether they enjoy its benefit or not. Otherwise, unless they received regeneration, they could never be saved, since without the rebirth through water and the Spirit, no one is granted entry into the kingdom of heaven.

And to the question whether, on account of God's intention, even hypocrites are allowed in the act of Baptism to labor under the vice of hypocrisy or cling in some other way to actual impenitence, so that, nevertheless, they are actually saved, Huber responds in the writing that he has disseminated that, if we do not allow this in any respect, we are not far away in this regard from the doctrine of Baptism taught by the Calvinists.

However, in order that they, too, may have our confession, we respond in this way: If in the act of Baptism some are hypocrites, which can easily happen, they are, indeed, regenerated, not with regard to something they have in their possession[57], but with regard to something they own[58] as far as God is concerned[59], which, as Luther says, is worked by immutable necessity. For everything essential was conferred on them. Hence, as many as were baptized, **all** are said to be buried together with Christ (Rom. 6). **And all** have been clothed with Christ (Gal. 3), where even as far as God is concerned it must necessarily take place. Otherwise, they would have received an

---

57   τῇ κρήσει
58   τῇ κτήσει
59   *quo ad Deum*

empty Baptism and a seal without its validity[60]. To assert such a thing is Calvinian to the highest degree, for thus Baptism is rent asunder with its essence removed from it. We call "essential" that word that gives adoption, that word with which God swears that He wants to consider and reckon the one who is baptized, not as a child of wrath, but now instead as a child of grace and an heir of eternal life. For this is regeneration, as far as God is concerned; our unbelief does not remove its reliability or the *effect* that it confers as something that is owned,[61] even though, according to Romans 3, one does not apply the use of it to himself. For it remains true, as far as God is concerned, that the baptized man was *reckoned* [62] as a *son and heir, truly absolved from sins, purged of natural defect, and at the same time the gifts of heavenly grace were furnished and poured out over him—whatever gifts pertain to adoption and regeneration.* These *are the essential things* in Baptism, and they are truly furnished to all the baptized. This is why, as far as God is concerned, all the baptized are truly said to be regenerated. If it were otherwise and it happened that a hypocrite wanted to repent 20 years later, he would certainly then have to be regenerated later, or else he could never enter the kingdom of heaven. If he is to be regenerated at a later date, and he was not regenerated at that earlier date, as far as the institution of God and its effect are concerned, then he will certainly have to be rebaptized. If he is not to be rebaptized, and nevertheless is regenerated after all those years, then Baptism has already been torn apart, and the essence of Baptism has been removed and subtracted from the act of Baptism and placed at an-

60   *veritate*
61   in κτήσει
62   *reputatum*

other time, as the Calvinists want to believe. If it should be said that through the Word a hypocrite can be regenerated after a certain interval of time, then that is proof that, by this doctrine, his entrance into the kingdom of heaven is made known *apart from rebirth, which takes place through water and* the Spirit, and that would be contrary to the institution of Christ (Mat. 3).

Thus far Huber's words.

We shall refute the rationale behind his assertion shortly, where previously we affirmed our own negative reasoning from the Word of God. Moreover, it is evident that hypocrites and the impenitent are not regenerated as long as they remain such, first, because regeneration cannot be separated or divorced from faith for even a moment, nor since the beginning of the world has anyone ever been regenerated who has not at the same time obtained faith at the time of his regeneration. But now, since hypocrites and the impenitent lack faith, they certainly also lack regeneration.

Next, regeneration signifies the transfer of those very men from a state of wrath to a state of grace. For this reason, they are proclaimed to be reborn, since those who were formerly children of wrath are now born as children of God. But none are children of God except for those who truly believe in Christ without hypocrisy (John 1).

In addition, regeneration, which the Holy Spirit effects when Baptism is undergone in faith, is combined with renewal. For it is said to be a washing not only of regeneration, but also of renewal in the Holy Spirit (Titus 3). But a renewal without the new movements of the Holy Spirit in the heart of a man neither exists nor can it be defined. Since these movements do not happen in hypocrites, certainly neither renewal nor the regeneration connected to it apply to them.

Furthermore, no one is reborn who is not justified. Those hypocrites are not among the justified, since they are devoid of justifying faith. Therefore, neither can they be ascribed to the regenerate—unless, perhaps, it is now permissible to fashion a third justification, so that hypocrites lose that first and general justification through unbelief; they do not have that particular[63] justification that is by faith, due to a deficiency of faith; and now, through Baptism, they acquire a sort of third justification which can stand beautifully together with unbelief, hypocrisy and impenitence.

In addition, all those things that the Scriptures proclaim about regeneration are so opposed to the impenitence of hypocrites that to place the gift of rebirth together with impenitence is tantamount to fabricating a union of light and darkness. Christ affirms in His dialogue with Nicodemus (John 3) that the entrance into the kingdom of heaven has been opened to the reborn. But we know that heaven still remains closed to hypocrites until they should repent and believe in Christ. The Lord teaches in the same place: "Just as the wind is discovered by its sound and blowing, so is *everyone* who is born of the Spirit," that is, his regeneration cannot remain hidden without the gentle whisper of the Holy Spirit being noticed in him, along with other fruits of conversion which would be exceedingly absurd to ascribe to those reprobate hypocrites. Thus, in John 1, faith coincides with rebirth. "He gave authority to become children of God—to those who believed in His name, who are born not of blood nor of the will of the flesh, nor of the will of a man, but born of God" (John 1). Thus John writes in his Epistle: "No one who is born of God commits sin," obviously demonstrating that to be born of God and to sin against conscience cannot coexist in the same person at one and the same time. Whence St. John most clearly defines what ought to be concluded about those hypocrites and impeni-

---

63   *specialem*

tent who sin on purpose and persevere in sins, namely, that they are not to be numbered among the reborn.

In the same Epistle John writes, chapter 5: "Whatever is born of God conquers the world, and this is the victory that conquers the world, our faith." The following argument is constructed from this:

Whatever is born of God conquers the world.

Hypocrites and all those without faith do not conquer the world, but remain under the power of the prince of this world, the devil.

Therefore, they are not born of God.

And observe that in this sentence, too, faith and regeneration are combined as things that are so closely linked to each other that they cannot in any way be torn apart from one another, either by intervals of time or even by proximity.

In the Book of Concord the meanings of the word "regeneration" are expressly unfolded. At times it is taken in the sense of embracing, at one and the same time, the remission of sins and the subsequent renewal. At other times, however, the word regeneration means only the remission of sins and the adoption as sons. Regeneration is also frequently used for sanctification and renewal (which follows justification by faith). None of these meanings applies to hypocrites, whether they are hypocrites at the time of their Baptism or afterwards. Therefore, even in this way Dr. Huber's dogma differs greatly not only from the Holy Scriptures, but also from the Book of Concord.

When Huber says that, in the Baptism of hypocrites which they receive at the time of their hypocrisy, regeneration is conferred on hypocrites as far as the work and institution of God are concerned, if he means to say that God truly instituted and destined Baptism for this, that they, too, should be regenerated, that is, with the obstacle of unbelief and impenitence removed, but that they are not regenerated because they put up a barrier (as they said once upon a time), then let Dr. Huber retain his interpretation and let him correct the text, that is, let him retain the meaning and fix the language.

For as soon as it is said, "This one or that one has been regenerated as far as God is concerned," it is immediately implied that the very act of regeneration was truly accomplished in him. If Huber, in fact, does not draw this conclusion regarding hypocrites, in whom regeneration is certainly by no means accomplished, then let him from now on do away with the ambiguous, dangerous, and indeed, literally and patently false phrases that he has been using, and let him be sure to keep the pattern of sound words, as one together with his colleagues.

Indeed, if regeneration pertained to the essence of Baptism (as Huber dreams), then surely all those on whom Baptism is conferred would also be regenerated by necessity. But Huber will never be able to prove that regeneration pertains to the essence of Baptism (we ascribe regeneration to the effects or the fruits of Baptism, according to Luther's Catechism), nor will he find any theologian who casts his vote with him in this matter. Therefore, if he plainly holds to this opinion, that those hypocrites are actually regenerated in Baptism on account of the intention of God (as he has said in private conversation); and that the work of regeneration (as his writing indicates) has been accomplished in them; and that regeneration is *conferred* on them; and that hypocrites, working under the vice of hypocrisy at the very time of their Baptism, are regenerated with regard to something they own[64]; then he must recognize that this opinion of his is

---

64   τῇ κτήσει

overturned by all these arguments that we have just enumerated.

Nor does the addition of that limitation, "as far as God is concerned," help him in the least. Otherwise, since Dr. Huber says that those unbelievers who are baptized in the midst of their wickedness are regenerated "as far as God is concerned," so he might also affirm that they are provided with faith "as far as God is concerned," since the divine intention in Baptism aims no less at this, that faith be conferred on a man, than that regeneration be conferred on him. But if the intention of God does not stretch to the point that the person who persists in impenitence is gifted with faith, then certainly it does not stretch to the point that they are regenerated. Indeed, what things might *not* be concluded from that intention of God? Doesn't the intention of God have as its final aim that a man be saved through Baptism (Titus 3, 1 Pet. 3)? Is a hypocrite saved, then? On the contrary, he is not saved but is damned all the more, and the judgment of the Lord presses down on him all the harder, because with a perverse heart he allows himself to be initiated with the Sacraments[65] of Christianity.

In Huber's first chapter on election, it becomes evident just how much chaos of absurdity arises from this form of argument, even with regard to the other areas of the Church's ministry. Yes, these are the things that Dr. Huber offers against us in the writing he has disseminated—things that are most definitely false and plainly contradictory. For what kind of rebirth is this that can stand together with unbelief and impenitence? Indeed, who would be so prodigiously foolish as to imagine that a hypocrite who undergoes Baptism with a wicked heart is reckoned by God as a son and heir, contrary to what is said in John 1: "He gave the authority to become children of God *to those who believed* in His name." How has the impenitent hypocrite been *truly absolved* from sins? How has he been *purged* from his native defect? How were the gifts of heavenly *grace* furnished to him and poured out over him—*whatever things* pertain *to adoption and regeneration*? These monstrous things are absolutely unheard of in the Churches of the Reformation[66].

We attribute the effect to God in the Baptism of the impenitent, but not the effect of regeneration. Rather it is the effect of *judgment and damnation*, as the *Refutation of Orthodox Consensus* testifies.[67]

The words of Paul that Huber cites in Rom. 6 and Gal. 3—we say that it is the fruit of Baptism, so that the baptized become participants in the death of Jesus Christ, and put on Christ in the way that the Apostle tells us there.

Now, surely we do not reject the distinction made by St. Augustine, who said: "Some put on Christ for the reception of the Sacrament; others, for sanctification of life." But what Huber means, that the hypocrites put on Christ fully for regeneration—that he will never be able to prove from the words of the Apostle.

For Dr. Huber twists Paul's words ("As many of you as were baptized have put on Christ") in order to concoct a regeneration even of those baptized whose heart is bound by iniquity and full of the venom of bitterness in the very act of Baptism. He does this in spite of the meaning of the Apostle, who limits his affirmation in such a way that he does not mean for it to be extended beyond baptized believers. "*All of you*," he says, "are sons of God for this reason, that *you have believed* in Christ Jesus. For as many of you as were baptized have put on Christ." Therefore, what Dr. Huber infers from this, that even hypocrites are regenerated or receive regeneration, and that it is conferred on them—that never entered the mind of the Apostle Paul.

66   *Ecclesiis reformatis*
67   *teste Refutatione Orthodoxi consensus*

But Dr. Huber is also mistaken in this: He writes that, "Unless hypocrites receive regeneration in Baptism, they can never be saved thereafter, since without the rebirth that takes place through water and the Spirit, no one is granted entry into the kingdom of heaven, and they cannot be rebaptized."

But he speaks as if God had no other means of regenerating and converting except for Baptism. But He does; He has the *Word*. For the Word, too, is an instrument of regeneration, as it is written in 1 Pet. 1, "You were born again, not of perishable seed, but of imperishable—through the living Word of God."

Indeed, St. Peter expressly says to Simon Magus, who was also thought to be a hypocrite, even though he had been baptized: "Turn from your malice and beg *God* that perhaps the thoughts of your heart may be forgiven you."

Therefore, if such a person can be turned to repentance through the Word, then even though Baptism was previously received without faith, he now begins to be converted for salvation, and he can take effective and firm comfort in it in all temptation.

For although the fruit of Baptism was, for a time, suspended and upset through hypocrisy and unbelief, nevertheless, since the Baptism itself, with regard to its essence, is a true and valid Baptism, and the promise of God attached to Baptism (that God wishes to be propitious to the man who is converted from sins to God by virtue of the one-time beginning of Baptism) does not vacillate or change on God's part, for that reason, whenever a man turns and is converted to *Christ Jesus*, he now finds in his Baptism the benefits deposited there, which he did not possess previously because of a lack of faith, that is, he finds the grace of God, remission of sins, adoption, and perpetual salvation.

Chapter IV: Concerning the Church

The forms of speech that Dr. Huber employs in the article on election have been arranged in such a way as to leave no theological passage concerning the Church intact or uncorrupted.

Up to the present time, the orthodox have always taught that salvation is not to be sought outside the Church,[68] just as long ago no one was saved from the waters of the Flood outside of Noah's ark. But how is it that salvation is not said to be outside the Church, if, by the assertions of the Huberian hypothesis, there is a certain general election, a general justification and remission of sins, a general adoption, etc., in which a special privilege is common, not only to the Church, but to all nations and unbelieving peoples—yes, to the whole world equally?

Fortunately, in urging against the papists that their visible Church is only distinguished by visible marks, our men have always argued here that the Church is considered in two ways. For the word "Church" refers either to the assembly of the called in which there are many hypocrites, just as the weeds and the chaff were, at one time, to be separated from the wheat; or the word "Church" refers properly to the invisible Church, which is the assembly of the truly believing and of those predestined to eternal life.

Dr. Luther approved this definition by John Hus (which was opposed by the papistic synagogue) as one of the sound articles which that holy martyr of God sealed as true with his blood.

---

68   *Extra Ecclesiam non esse quaerendam salutem*

But if all men together were elected to eternal life, then that distinction that has opposed the papists until now is most carelessly obscured and weakened.

In addition, the article from the Apostle's Creed is more than slightly obscured by Dr. Huber's doctrine. "I believe in the holy Church." All teachers up to the present time have judged that the label of "holiness" is a sign that separates this special people on earth from the rest who are not holy, from the unbelievers.

But what else is Dr. Huber doing by accommodating this title of holiness even to the pagan nations that are entirely ignorant *of God and of Christ*, than foolishly confusing the Church *of Christ* with the synagogue of Satan—yes, with Turks, Jews and Gentiles? In order that we may not appear to be trying to wrongly accuse him of anything, let us recall his own words. In the book dedicated to the German people of Amberg, pages 168-169, he writes thus:

> This is found (in the Scriptures), as the adversaries concede—or rather, as they are forced to concede, that God calls them "elect" whom He elsewhere calls "His beloved," or whom He has redeemed from the fall of Adam through His Son. Indeed, here the Holy Scriptures make *no distinction* among men, wherever and to whomever the Apostles have preached the Gospel *of Christ*, in whom the redemption of the world is contained. For they are *all* and *individually* called *beloved* of the Lord, *sanctified*, redeemed, *elected*.

And then:

> As truly as God, in His Son, established the reconciliation with the whole world, and as true as it was that Christ died for the salvation of all men, so it was also

true that God, *in* His Son, loved *all* of those very same people and redeemed them from Adam's fall, and *elected* them to His grace and chose them for Himself in their election. For all this glory exists in Christ, and *the human race* acquires it from Him, for it is called an *elect and priestly* race of God.

Thus far Dr. Huber.

This argument is defeated by its own ruling that the passage from Peter ("You are a chosen people, a royal priesthood") applies to the whole world and to all the men, nations and peoples on the planet. For it is certain that the words there apply only to the Church. For after the Apostle discusses the wicked world—how it rejected the cornerstone, Jesus Christ—he then submits by way of antithesis: "But you are a chosen race, a royal priesthood, a holy nation, a people that has come into possession, that you may proclaim the virtues of Him who called you out of darkness into His marvelous light."

The antithesis indicated here demonstrates that Peter is applying these words to the Christians and to the true Church, and is most clearly separating and distinguishing it from those who rejected the cornerstone, Jesus Christ. This antithesis alone ought to subdue Huber's audacity, so that he would not attribute that praise that belongs to the saints also to those whom Peter excludes from it by way of a striking contrast. This is also clear in that the Apostle Peter repeats the words of Moses about the "chosen nation" and the "royal priesthood," by which titles God once taught that the people of Israel had been claimed by God ahead of all the other nations as His own possession (Exo. 19). Peter now applies this to the Christians of the New Testament in the kingdom of Christ. The argument that Peter is here thinking of the Church and not of the unbelieving peoples is aided also in that he called them a *holy* nation, attributing a title of this kind that, as the context of this article of the Apostles' Creed indicates, is reserved for the Church. The final proof of this argument is that he calls them a people who have been called out of darkness into the light of God, while the unbelieving peoples are still enveloped in their darkness, nor does the light of the Gospel of the glory of Christ enlighten them (Isa. 9 and 2 Cor. 4).

Since we discussed it above, we will omit here the fact that he ascribes the introduction to the Epistle to the Ephesians (where it mentions those who are elect and adopted as sons) to the entire human race. To be sure there is hardly any excuse for that corruption with which the introduction to the First Epistle to the Corinthians was distorted and related to the whole world (and thus even to the unbelieving Gentiles). Orthodox writers have previously been accustomed to extracting the definition of the Church from this very introduction.

For thus Huber writes on page 172 of the writing dedicated to the people of Amberg:

> If we consider the aid of God and the love He has declared for all men, then not only are *all men* named the elect of God before the foundations of the world according to grace, but they are also called the beloved of God, *the sanctified* of God.

And to these words Dr. Huber notes in the margin the same Epistle and chapter, namely, 1 Corinthians 1.

But the utterly clear context of the words of Paul demonstrates more brilliantly than the sun that Paul is dedicating his Epistle, not to the Gentiles who were not yet converted to the knowledge of *Christ*, but (as the words plainly say), to the Church of God that is in Corinth, to the sanctified. Paul himself uses this title in the same Epistle, chapter 6, to refer to the converted and to the Christians who had been sanctified from sins, saying: "Neither fornicators, etc., will receive the inheritance of the kingdom of God. And that, indeed, is what you were. But you were washed. But you were sanctified. But you were justified through the name of the Lord Jesus and through the Spirit of our God." But Paul adds in his address, "To the called saints." Therefore, he is dealing with saints who are within the assembly of the called, not outside of it. Again he adds: "…together with all those who call upon the name of our Lord *Jesus Christ* in whatever place, whether theirs or ours." So there he is not dealing at all with those who do not call upon the name *of Christ.* In fact, in the fifth chapter, after he had rebuked them for fornication and other shameful acts, he expressly adds: "For what do I have to do with judging even those who are outside? Are you not to judge those who are on the inside? Indeed, God judges those who are on the outside. Expel him who is evil from your midst."

These and other things teach quite clearly that the address of the Pauline Epistle pertains to the Church and not to the unbelieving Gentiles in the world. Indeed, that title "sanctified" is attributed to the assembly of the called only because of the presence of the elect in that assembly and does not apply to the hypocrites themselves, but only to the truly believing, just as the designation "crop" applies, not to the weeds or the chaff, but to the wheat, for as much as the chaff may be interspersed with the wheat.

Nor is it that we think that these things that have been said just now about the Church are trivial matters, nor are we particularly interested in fighting over how someone interprets the sayings that have been enumerated. Indeed, if someone is pleased to use interpretations of this kind to weaken those addresses of the Epistles to the Corinthians and the Ephesians, or that notable passage from Peter ("You are a chosen nation, etc.")

whence the doctrine of the Church has, until now, been drawn and explained, then what stands in the way of allowing him to twist the other sayings concerning the Church, whenever they occur in the Scriptures, and apply them toward unbelieving peoples as well? Indeed, what is to prevent him from simply pulling down the boundaries of the Church and then creating a single kingdom out of the two realms, of God and of Satan, especially if a general election, remission of sins, justification and sanctification are attributed also to those who are subjects of Satan's kingdom?

In the same way, he now manifestly begins to apply the address of Peter's First Epistle also to the unbelieving peoples, that is, to the whole world, since Peter writes to the elect according to the foreknowledge of God the Father, although he is clearly describing the elect in this way, that they have been *regenerated* in a living hope, into an inheritance preserved for them in heaven, that they are guarded by God's power through faith for salvation, that they are about to obtain the goal of faith, the salvation of their souls.

Indeed, Huber's audacity breaks in, for he does not hesitate to explain the words of Paul in 2 The. 2 concerning the election of absolutely all men. There the Apostle most clearly separates the elect from the reprobate, saying: "But we (that is, we who do not so approve injustice and deception, like those wicked men whom I just now mentioned) ought to give thanks to God always concerning you, brothers loved by the Lord, because God elected you from the beginning for salvation through the *sanctification* of the Spirit and through *faith* in the truth, to which *He called* you through our Gospel, etc."

To wish to accommodate this pericope to the entire human race—this pericope that deals with the beloved in the Lord, with those who have the sanctification of the Spirit and faith in the truth, with those who have been called by the Gospel—and thus also to unbelieving peoples and individuals, is not only extremely ignorant, but extremely demented. Dr. Huber's recent letters show that he does this repeatedly. He scatters these letters around constantly and sets forth in broad daylight the many errors and absurdities that proceed from the beatings of his heart.

Nor is what Dr. Huber asserts true: that wherever the Apostles went, wherever the Gospel would be preached, they indiscriminately called all men *beloved* of God or sanctified.

For the distinction has already been made, and Dr. Huber's assertion is also refuted by the Book of the Acts of the Apostles. For when Paul came to the Jews who feared and honored God, he greeted them as brothers, especially since they were also his brothers according to the flesh, born from the same nation. When, in turn, he came to the nations that were not yet converted and still mere unbelievers, no such titles are read there like the Apostles employed in their introductions when they wrote to the churches. This is clear in the first two sermons to those in Lystra (Acts 14) and to the Athenians (Acts 17).

Huber roars that these titles, according to their *proper* meaning, refer to the counsel of God and to His mercy, which the Apostles were proclaiming to all indiscriminately. If this objection were at all valid, then wouldn't it be equally permissible to call even the Gentiles who were not yet converted "converted, illumined, blessed, saved" and anything else?

Huber argues that our meaning cannot be correct when we say that the opening addresses of the Epistles had the application of faith in view, for then the Apostles could not have called those to whom they were writing "saints" and "sanctified" and "elect," because they were not able to search the hearts of men, nor to see which of them would still be believing in the end.

I respond: They didn't need to see into anyone's heart or peer into the future. Nevertheless, these titles were entirely appropriate, because they undoubtedly knew that wherever the Church has been gathered through the Word, there some of the elect and true believers and the sanctified are always present, because the Word of God does not fall in vain, nor does it return empty (Isa. 55).

To summarize briefly, we must distinguish between a general and inclusive[69] recognition on the one hand, and an exclusive[70] recognition on the other. According to an inclusive recognition, the Apostles knew that wherever the Church—the assembly of the called—is, there some of the elect are present. But according to an exclusive recognition, they did not know for certain and beyond a doubt which individuals truly believed in Christ and had, at length, obtained salvation, although they might judge quite well by the fruits of faith shown by some. Indeed, the Apostles themselves ascribed this exclusive recognition not to themselves, but to God and to the Prince of shepherds, Jesus Christ, saying: "The Lord knows those who are His" (2 Tim. 2).

Therefore, from the things that have been dealt with thus far, it is most evident that Huber favors and fights for such a doctrine that has been concocted from a mixture of Schwenkfeldianism, Papism, the madness of the Anabaptists, and Puccianism. It smacks of Schwenkfeldianism because he alleges that even those peoples who do not have the Word or the Sacraments have been sanctified and justified without means, apart from the Word and Sacraments. It reeks of Papism because he thinks that no one can be certain of the final outcome of persevering until the end. It is Anabaptist, because it necessarily follows from his general justification and sanctification that men are born saints and justified, even before they are baptized. Finally, his argu-

69   *generalem et confusam*
70   *discretam*

ments coincide with the Puccian madness, since both sides employ the same fundamental arguments, although they aim at a different goal.[71]

For this reason, unless Dr. Huber recognizes and abandons his improper usages[72] in the article of predestination; and afterwards, sacredly and religiously guards the pattern of sound words; and then, with a genuine recantation, retracts the remaining errors of universal justification, the sanctification of all peoples and unbelieving nations, the regeneration of hypocrites, etc.; we testify before God and Christ, the Judge of all, that we cannot maintain peace and fraternity with him.

THE END

<hr>

71   *ad diversum scopum tendant*
72   *acyrologies*